BLACK BOOKS GALORE!
Guide to Great African American Children's Books
about Boys

Other Black Books Galore! Titles

The Black Books Galore! Guide to Great African American Children's Books

The Black Books Galore! Guide to Great African American Children's Books about Girls

Black Books Galore!

Guide to
Great African American
Children's Books
about Boys

Donna Rand

Toni Trent Parker

John Wiley & Sons, Inc.
New York • Chichester • Weinheim • Brisbane • Singapore • Toronto

This book is printed on acid-free paper. ♾

Published by John Wiley & Sons, Inc.
Published simultaneously in Canada

Design and production by Navta Associates, Inc.

Permissions and credits begin on page 207.

This publication is designed to provide accurate and authoritative information in regard to the subject matter covered. It is sold with the understanding that the publisher is not engaged in rendering professional services. If professional advice or other expert assistance is required, the services of a competent professional person should be sought.

Library of Congress Cataloging-in-Publication Data:
Rand, Donna.
    Black Books Galore! guide to great African American children's books about boys / by
Donna Rand, Toni Trent Parker.
        p.   cm.
    Includes indexes.
    ISBN 0–471–37527–6 (pbk.)
    1. Afro-Americans—Juvenile literature—Bibliography.   2. Children's literature,
American—Afro-American authors—Bibliography.   3. Afro-American boys—Books and
reading.   4. Afro-American boys—Juvenile literature—Bibliography.   5. Boys in literature—
Bibliography.   I. Title: Guide to great African American children's books about boys.
II. Parker, Toni Trent.   III. Black Books Galore!   IV. Title.
Z1361.N39 R336   2000
[E185]
016.97304'96073—dc21   00–042257

Printed in the United States of America
10 9 8 7 6 5 4 3 2 1

To my dear son, Christopher,
with all my love!

D. R.

To the next generation of readers:
David, Max, Hank, Brian II, Luke, and Wendell

T. T. P.

Contents

Acknowledgments

WE HAVE BEEN BLESSED with a number of friends and family members who have enthusiastically supported us in the preparation of this book.

First and foremost, we thank our own family members, Barry, Christopher, and Allison Rand; and Danny, Christine, Kathleen, and Jennifer Parker, for their patience and active support.

We would like to acknowledge and thank our friend and former partner, Sheila Foster, for her original vision of Black Books Galore!

We extend our appreciation and kudos to Danny Parker, who generously donated his personal time to act as our photographer. His results speak for themselves.

Thanks also to those families who took the time to pose for photos. We appreciate the Strong, Dudley Williams, Herb Williams, Perry, Collins, Mayfield, Tookes, and McDonald families.

We have always enjoyed working with a number of talented authors and illustrators who always stand ready to support our projects. We would like to thank Gavin Curtis, Sharon Draper, Tom Feelings, Eloise Greenfield, Patricia Mignon Hinds, Angela Johnson, Dolores Johnson, Julius Lester, Cedric Lucas, Patricia McKissack, Robert Miller, Walter Dean Myers, Denise Lewis Patrick, Harriette Gillem Robinet, Synthia Saint James, Irene Smalls, and Mildred Pitts Walter for their participation in this book.

And we wish to thank Dr. Barbara Thrash Murphy, author of *Black Authors and Illustrators of Books for Children and Young Adults: A Biographical Dictionary,* for her assistance in networking with several of our featured authors and illustrators.

Likewise, we were deeply gratified by the supportive comments offered by Ed Bradley, Doug E. Doug, Dr. Benjamin Carson, Hugh Price, A. Barry Rand, Kenneth Chenault, and Earl G. Graves Sr. that appear in this book.

We have enjoyed working with the talented publishing professionals at John Wiley & Sons and wish to express our sincere appreciation to our editor, Carole Hall; Marcia Samuels, our managing editor; and the production staff who masterfully put it all together.

Introduction

WE ARE PLEASED to offer this annotated guide to 350 books about the lives and adventures of African American boys and men.

The stories we have selected are about little boys, adolescent boys, and grown men; about young boys and old men; about real people, some of whom are performers, pioneers, athletes, and inventors; and about fictitious characters who are, among other things, doctors, teachers, students, slaves, sons, fathers, brothers, and friends. What do they all have in common? They are wonderful black males whose stories can entertain, educate, and enrich young readers—especially African American boys, from infants to young teens.

Why Books for Boys?

Different children have different needs, and generally speaking boys have different needs and interests than girls. For example, most experts have found that boys are not as interested in reading as girls are. We don't totally agree with that. It seems that the lines between boys and girls have blurred in recent years. Both boys and girls are involved in a lot more extracurricular activities, are engrossed in television, and rely on computer and video games for their entertainment. But we do agree that you can increase the odds of interesting a young boy in books. How do you do that? You find books, like the ones in this guide, that appeal to a young boy's interests and enhance his sense of self-worth.

About Our Selections

Each Black Books Galore! selection portrays a positive, active male character. The characters are attractive, bright, thoughtful, strong, resourceful, and capable, and they are always the focal point of the stories. Your boy reader will recognize himself or relate to the characters within the stories and see visions of himself, through illustrations that look like him and his family and friends.

> "**I**mages—strong, proud and happy, brave, and now also humorous. . . . What a joy it is to see black faces of all shades in our children's books. If only my favorite book, *The Giving Tree,* by Shel Silverstein, had a black character, I would picture myself as the little boy that grew to value friendship over money. I had to learn that one the hard way. Thank God, our children will not!"
>
> **Doug E. Doug**
> *Actor,* The Bill Cosby Show

We have carefully selected books of every possible genre, and from a diverse group of authors and illustrators representing a wide range of styles. Our selections include a variety of picture and story books to engage small children, and a plethora of nonfiction books, chapter books, and novels intended for more mature young readers. It is important to note that the overwhelming number of these selections are about boys doing what boys do, without regard to their race. There are many, many stories about boys as friends; boys in conflict; boys in sports; boys in families; boys playing, singing, dancing; and boys in a variety of adventure situations. So, these books are largely about boyhood experiences, not just African American boyhood experiences.

The selections include, but are certainly not limited to, many books in each of the following special categories.

Pioneers and Cowboys

Traditionally, young boys love to read about the raucous adventures of pioneers and cowboys of the Old West. Yet many young African American boys may not understand the extent of blacks' participation in the western story. We have included an entertaining and educational selec-

> "**A**s a young athlete and avid sports fan I read everything I could about African American sports heroes such as Jackie Robinson, Joe Lewis, Jesse Owens, and others, who not only achieved greatness in their respective sports, but who were also real and symbolic representations of black excellence. I understood at a very early age that when given the opportunity, blacks, in whatever field, would excel, just as these determined athletes had. I was motivated and inspired by their stories. I realized that their athletic accomplishments were more than just that—they were important precursors to greater social change."
>
> **A. Barry Rand** *Chairman and Chief Executive Officer, Avis Group*

tion of books like *Bill Pickett: Rodeo-Ridin' Cowboy* [98], *Wagon Wheels* [247], *The Longest Ride* [309], the very endearing *The Righteous Revenge of Artemis Bonner* [326], and others, which are both true and fictional accounts of those adventurous times.

Folktales and Legends

Folktales and legends are not only entertaining, very often they have important lessons to impart. We have included a number of pleasing folktales from the African and American caches that teach important virtues. Consider offering your boy readers *Anansi Finds a Fool* [89] or *Nobiah's Well: A Modern African Folktale* [202] for folktales from the African storytelling tradition, or *John Henry* [156], *Sam and the Tigers: A New Retelling of Little Black Sambo* [220], or *Little Muddy Waters: A Gullah Folk Tale* [173] to introduce him to traditional, American tales.

Biographies

The life stories and contributions of African Americans have been largely lost in a vacuum of denial. Yet there are so many intriguing biographical stories about blacks who have contributed significantly to American history. It is easy to find books about important African American figures like Martin Luther King Jr. or Frederick Douglass. But young boys should also read books like *My Name Is York* [194] to learn about the slave who helped guide the Lewis and Clark expedition; *The Real McCoy: The Life of an African American Inventor* [217] to learn about the black inventor who revolutionized the rail industry with his single invention; or books about Tiger Woods, Grant Hill, or Emmitt Smith, all contemporary sports stars with fascinating stories. Other selections offer energizing insights into the lives of African American male jurists, writers, athletes, entertainers, and others.

"As a youngster I enjoyed reading autobiographies by black men and women who dedicated themselves to righting wrongs and breaking down barriers so that the people who came after them could step forward and have better lives. Books like *Up from Slavery* by Booker T. Washington, *The Narrative of Sojourner Truth,* and *The Narrative of the Life of Frederick Douglass* inspired me to make part of my life's work finding ways to make a difference . . . to bring about a positive change in society.

"I believe that whatever level of success African Americans enjoy today, however hard we worked to get there, we did not do it alone. We individually and collectively are part of a continuum of effort to break down barriers and bring about positive social change. I learned this lesson as a child from reading the travails and triumphs of great men and women like Frederick Douglass, Sojourner Truth, and Booker T. Washington."

Kenneth Chenault
President & Chief Operating Officer, American Express Company

History and Heritage

While the sum and substance of the African American experience is much more than slavery, we have included many stories of historical fiction about young men who were slaves, like *Ajeemah and His Son* [264], *Silent Thunder: A Civil War Story* [330], *Big Jabe* [96], and others. These stories are important because they express deeper truths about the slave condition, and because the young men in these stories demonstrate their humanity, spirit, intellect, innovation, and strength of character, all attributes not often ascribed to slave people.

Sports

There are plenty of books included about sports and players that will capture the attention of young boy readers. From nonfiction selections like *Leagues Apart: The Men and Times of the Negro Baseball Leagues* [169] and *Black Hoops: The History of African Americans in Basketball* [271] to fictional stories like those offered in the Patrick's Pals series about the young Patrick Ewing and his friends, or the poems in *Red Dog, Blue Fly: Football Poems* [324], there is something for every young sports fan. There is even a compelling story about a young golfer in *Night Golf* [201].

What About the Women and Girls?

Of course, boys and men do not live in a vacuum, so girls and women are featured in supporting roles in many of our selections. They are the mothers, grandmothers, daughters, sisters, and friends of our heroes, so we have taken equal care to ensure that they are also well depicted as strong, capable people, avoiding sexist representations. The whole point of this guide is to engage young African American boys in books that also offer them a positive view of their world. By the way, even though these books are primarily about boy characters, we highly recommend them for girls, too.

About Black Books Galore!

Our expertise in African American children's books began with our personal interest, as parents, in finding appropriate, positive books for our own children. We started a small business in 1992 with a very large mission. We dedicated ourselves to identifying and distributing fine African American children's books. Since we began, we have found over 1,600 appropriate titles for and about African American children.

We have happily shared our annotated book list, in this and other Black Books Galore! guides, as a way of helping parents and educators find them for their children and students. However, since we are neither professional educators nor librarians, we have remained true to our original role. Therefore, we recommend these books for your boy readers only as parents. We have read and reviewed every selection and have only included books that we would give to our own sons.

"As a child, I lived to read books. They were a pathway to worlds and people far from my neighborhood in Philadelphia. They exposed me to different people, cultures, ideas, and adventures. Because there were virtually no books with black characters, it was left to my imagination to think that some of those worlds and adventures might open to me."

Ed Bradley
Correspondent, 60 Minutes

"I had several books that I enjoyed as a child, but no real favorites. I wish there had been more books that reflected my world and my interests. It would have been great if there were books like the Black Stars series that told children about African American entrepreneurs and inventors. Those are the types of books that would have really captivated me as a kid. Who knows, I might have even started my business sooner if I had been able to read about black men and women who had done the same."

Earl G. Graves Sr.
Chairman, Publisher, and Chief Executive Officer,
Black Enterprise *magazine, Earl Graves Ltd.*

The book selections are classified by age group, with story lines and concepts that are age appropriate. You, of course, are the final judge regarding your child's maturity and reading level.

"When I was a child growing up, there were few books that had black characters or black children in them, and I certainly believe that it would have been useful to see some black people in a very positive role. My favorite books as a child, in retrospect, were Bible stories such as *Uncle Arthur's Bedtime Stories*, as well as specific stories from the Bible. I also greatly enjoyed reading stories that featured animals as the main characters. Certainly as far as the animal books are concerned, it wouldn't have mattered whether they were black characters or not.

"It is unfortunate that I was unable to learn as a child about such people as Elijah McCoy, who had so many inventions that there is now a famous phrase named after him—'the real McCoy.' I certainly would have been very interested to know that the traffic signal had been invented by a black man, named Garrett Morgan, who also invented the gas mask. There are numerous other examples, particularly in the medical field, of great contributions by black Americans that totally eluded me as a child. Nevertheless, because I ultimately believe that the only important thing is a relationship with God, it didn't bother me as much as it would have, had I not had that perspective.

"I am extremely happy that there are books around now like the series from Zondervan called Today's Heroes. These feature heroic figures of all nationalities and certainly have had a positive impact on many of the black children that I have encountered. There are also a whole host of picture books featuring black children and adults now, which I think are extremely worthwhile in terms of helping young black children formulate identities about themselves during their developmental stages. I am very glad that the Black Books Galore! guides to great African American children's books are available."

Benjamin S. Carson Sr., M.D.
Professor and Director of Pediatric Neurosurgery,
Johns Hopkins Medical Institutions

How to Use This Guide

THE MAIN ENTRIES of this guide have been organized into three parts, which list books appropriate for the following reading levels:

- Babies and preschoolers
- Early readers (kindergarten to grade 3)
- Middle readers (grades 4 to 8)

The titles in each part are arranged alphabetically. All the entries are numbered sequentially, from 1 to 350, for easy cross-referencing. Throughout the book, numbers appearing in brackets, such as [257], refer to entry numbers, not page numbers.

Each numbered entry includes the title, subtitle, author and illustrator, the publisher of the hardcover and softcover editions, the original publication date of the book, and a brief synopsis of book. We have also noted significant awards and listed any sequel, prequel, companion, or series titles for your reference.

There are several books in this guide that contain nonstandard English, in either black or Caribbean dialect. There is a school of thought that suggests that these books have cultural and literary significance and that the language, when used in the context of the character, place, and time, is appropriate. Others believe that reading nonstandard English is counterproductive to a child's language development. Rather than making that decision for you, we have clearly identified books that contain significant passages of nonstandard English or Caribbean dialect, or "Use of N Word," in case of the use of the derogatory racial slur, for your consideration.

"The Creator's Reflections" and Other Special Features

Pictures of book covers and text excerpts from many of the selections are placed throughout to better impart the flavor of the books. Additionally, seventeen talented authors and illustrators are spotlighted in "The Creator's Reflections." Each creator offers a retrospective reflection on their favorite childhood books and their views of children's books today. In the main entries, the names of these featured artists are followed by a ☆ and the page number on which their reflections appear. Here is a complete list of the creators:

There are four indexes to help you find what you want or to browse: an index of titles, which lists each entry and the titles of any other books mentioned within the entries; an index of authors; an index of illustrators; and an index of topics.

How to Get Your Hands on the Books in This Guide

The books in this guide should be available through your school or public library, or at a bookstore. There are a number of African American specialty bookstores throughout the country whose staffs may be very knowledgeable about these and other books and who may be able to supply these titles for you easily. If they are still in print, you should be able to order them through your local bookseller. To find or order your selection, you should have the title and the author's name.

Libraries may be able to accommodate your special requests. If they do not have the book you want in their own system, they may be able to borrow it through an interlibrary loan arrangement.

And of course, you can always contact us, Black Books Galore!, at 65 High Ridge Rd, #407, Stamford, CT 06905. Phone 203-359-6925, Fax 203-359-3226, Web site, www.blackbooksgalore.com to order your selection of African American children's books. Please enclose a self-addressed, stamped, business-size envelope if you would like a response to an inquiry.

Books for
Babies and Preschoolers

RAISING A LITTLE BOY from a baby to a young adult is an awesome responsibility. He arrives with a clean slate, ready to absorb and process everything and anything that he sees, hears, and feels. For too brief a time, you have the governing hand in his exposure to the world.

Before outside influences begin to exert themselves, it is your job to be sure his early impressions give him a positive sense of identity. That's where great children's books fit in. There you will find millions of impressions with which to guide him intellectually, socially, emotionally, and spiritually.

From the time your little boy is a baby, begin exposing him to books that may help counteract unfortunate stereotypes. It is not too early to start building his sense of himself as a strong, compassionate, responsible, supportive, and worthy human being. We have selected eighty-five books for this age group that offer building blocks to help him establish that sense through reading about other African American boys.

By preschool, your young boy is beginning to assess himself against the rest of the world. He is tuning in to the social cues that define what it means to be a male, especially a black male. He is also noticing female behavior, attitudes, and roles. Offering him African American children's books is a simple way to begin a more positive socialization process.

Many of the story lines in our selections are fantastical adventures that offer more than the traditional rough-and-tumble stories often written for boys. *Bear on a Bike* [5], *Big Boy* [7], *Kofi and the Butterflies* [53], and *Dave and the Tooth Fairy* [19] all depict little boys in wonderfully imaginative tales that can only expand a young boy's horizons.

We have also recommended a number of books that introduce positive stories of bonding between the generations—grandfathers, fathers, and sons. Books like *Father and Son* [27], *When I Am Old with You* [82], and *Grandfather and I* [34] portray black men as loving, committed role models to their sons. Other books, such as *Ben Makes a Cake* [6], *Jamal's Busy Day* [48], and *Daddy and I* [15], belie the traditional male role, portraying men doing housework, cooking, and cleaning as part of their family responsibility.

Of course, there are also several books about the special relationship that exists between mothers and their sons. *Jonathan and His Mommy* [50], *Jafta's Mother* [46], *Hanging Out with Mom* [38], and *Uh-oh! It's Mama's Birthday!* [80] are all charming stories demonstrating love and respect for the women in these young boys' lives.

There are also a number of books about black males in unexpected roles. As a young boy is studying his Bible, what treasured memories he will have of *Noah* [63] and other biblical characters found in *Climbing Jacob's Ladder* [14] as black men. And he will be amused envisioning that *Rumplestiltskin* [70] is a little black man.

It is exciting to think that sharing a simple early childhood book with a young boy can serve him so well. Not only are you exposing him to the concept of reading, but with these books you will also plant the seeds of self-esteem and self-confidence that will bloom through his life.

Animal Sounds for Baby [1]

Written by Cheryl Willis Hudson
Illustrated by George Ford

Board Book: Cartwheel, Scholastic
Published 1995

A toddler visits a petting zoo, where he makes fast friends with all of the farm animals and learns to imitate their unique sounds. Other titles in the What-A-Baby series include *Good Morning Baby, Good Night Baby* [33], and *Let's Count Baby.*

The Baby [2]

Written by Monica Greenfield
Illustrated by Jan Spivey Gilchrist

Board Book: HarperFestival, HarperCollins
Published 1994

A baby's daily routine of eating, kicking, crying, sleeping, and then eating again—all under the watchful eye of his mother—is pictured in this story of Baby's day.

Baby Says [3]

Written and illustrated by John Steptoe

Hardcover and softcover: Lothrop, Lee & Shepard, William Morrow
Published 1988

A baby, restricted to his playpen, tries everything he can to get his big brother's attention. Baby knows only two phrases, "Uh, oh," and "No, no," which his affectionate big brother uses to communicate with him. When the big brother is finally ready to help the little one out of the playpen, he says, "Okay, Baby, okay." Little ones will enjoy this book, especially if the baby talk is done with dramatic voice inflections.

Baby's Bedtime [4]

Written by Nikki Grimes
Illustrated by Sylvia Walker

Board Book: Western
Published 1995

A sleepy baby is bathed and prepared for bed by his loving parents. The illustrations of the baby and his doting daddy are especially heartwarming. Four other titles, *Baby's Colors, No Diapers for Baby, I Can Count* [40], and *Peekaboo Baby,* are in this series produced in cooperation with *Essence* magazine to celebrate young African American children.

Bear on a Bike [5]

Written by Stella Blackstone
Illustrated by Debbie Harter

Hardcover: Barefoot Beginners
Published 1998

This book has all of the elements to make it popular with young toddlers. The text is lyrical, with a catchy repeated phrase, and the illustrations are bright and whimsical. The story follows the escapades of a young boy and a bear who takes him on fantastic adventures to a castle, a forest, a beach, an island, and more.

Ben Makes a Cake [6]

Written by Verna Allette Wilkins
Illustrated by Helen Clipson

Softcover: Tamarind
Published 1987

A bright-faced eight-year-old boy named Ben is a cake-making expert and aspiring chef. One Sunday morning, his mother asks him to make a cake for guests who are coming for tea. Ben considers the dozens of mouth-watering cakes and tarts that he could make and the ingredients that he will need. Ben will, of course, need a grown-up to help him with the oven, but other than that, he is on his own!

Big Boy [7]

Written by Tololwa M. Mollel
Illustrated by E. B. Lewis

Hardcover: Clarion
Published 1995

Young Oli is sad because he isn't big enough to go hunting with his big brother. Instead, he has to take a nap, which he has no intention of doing. The young boy sneaks out of the house and climbs up a tree, where he comes face to face with Tunukia-Zawadi, the magical bird that can grant any wish. Oli overstates his wish, asking the bird to make him "as big as a mountain and as strong as the wind." Instantly Oli is transformed into a giant of a boy, but being so big is more difficult than Oli ever imagined. If only he could be small again. If only . . .

Big Friend, Little Friend [8]

Written by Eloise Greenfield ☆ 42
Illustrated by Jan Spivey Gilchrist

Board Book: Black Butterfly
Published 1991

A little boy enjoys the friendship and companionship of both an older child and a younger one. He is cared for by his older friend and in turn nurtures the younger one. The colorful illustrations show the children teaching and helping one another. Other books in this series include *Daddy and I* [15], *I Make Music,* and *My Doll Keshia.*

Billy's Boots: A First Lift-the-Flap Book [9]

Written by Debbie MacKinnon
Illustrated by Anthea Sieveking

Board Book: Dial, Penguin USA
Published 1996

Baby Billy is pictured on the front cover in his overalls and red boots. In eight delightful board pages, Billy searches for those boots. Young readers can actually flip open the diaper bag, closet door, and chest of drawers in this interactive book to help Billy find his boots.

Bringing the Rain to Kapiti Plain [10]

Written by Verna Aardema
Illustrated by Beatriz Vidal

Hardcover and softcover: Dial
Published 1981

This story is about a young African herdsman, Ki-pat, who shot an arrow into a cloud to bring rain down onto the drought-stricken plains. The text was adapted to the cadence of the familiar "House that Jack Built," and shares its cumulative refrain, which builds from verse to verse. Young children love both rhymes and rhythms, which are paired nicely in this delightful poem.

Charlie Parker Played Be Bop [11]

Written and illustrated
by Chris Raschka

Reading Rainbow Review Book

Hardcover: Orchard
Published 1992

Have fun with this book of auditory delights about the music that comes out of Charlie Parker's saxophone. When read with the right intonations, the jazz sounds, "Be Bop, Fisk Fisk, Lollipop, Boomba, Boomba," and more will delight young readers. After a while they are bound to read or even sing along.

Charlie's House [12]

Written by Reviva Schermbrucker
Illustrated by Niki Daly

Hardcover: Viking Penguin
Published 1991

A young South African boy, Charlie, builds a model house for his family from mud, sticks, and cardboard scraps, imagining that it is the house of his dreams. In his imagination, the rooms are big and include a living room, a bedroom for his mother and granny, and even a room for himself. Charlie's dream is shattered by the reality that he lives in a shanty made of leaky scrap-metal siding.

Chidi Only Likes Blue: An African Book of Colors [13]

Written and photographed by Ifeoma Onyefulu

Hardcover: Cobblehill
Published 1997

Nneka's little brother, Chidi, loves the color blue because it is the only color he knows, so Nneka decides to teach him the names of other colors. Using objects in their African village, Nneka shows Chidi examples of red, found in the special *igwe* (cap) worn by the village chiefs; yellow, in the *gari* (cassava grain) that they eat; and black, in the *uli* (seed paint) that they use to paint the village homes. Young readers will learn their colors as well as something about Africa through the photographs of the village and people. There are three companion books: *A Is for Africa, Emeka's Gift: An African Counting Story* [22], *Grandfather's Work: A Traditional Healer in Nigeria* [35], and *Ogbo: Sharing Life in an African Village.*

Climbing Jacob's Ladder: Heroes of the Bible in African-American Spirituals [14]

Selected by John Langstaff
Illustrated by Ashley Bryan

Hardcover: Margaret K. McElderry Books, Simon & Schuster
Published 1991

Nine Old Testament characters are praised in song in this colorful music book. The story of each black biblical hero is briefly presented and illustrated with bright paintings. Piano music and song lyrics are included for each character, among them the well-known "Rocka My Soul" about Abraham and the spirited "Didn't It Rain?" about Noah.

Daddy and I [15]

Written by Eloise Greenfield ☆ 42
Illustrated by Jan Spivey Gilchrist

Board Book: Black Butterfly, Writers and Readers
Published 1991

Daddy and son are pictured doing household chores together in this heart-warming story. Their chores include everything from painting to doing the laundry, which sets a wonderful example of family responsibility for little boys! This book has three companion titles—*Big Friend, Little Friend* [8]; *I Make Music;* and *My Doll Keshia*—by the same author and illustrator.

Daddy Calls Me Man [16]

Written by Angela Johnson ☆ 64
Illustrated by Rhonda Mitchell

Hardcover: Orchard
Published 1997

A very young boy is colorfully portrayed in vibrant illustrations of four poems written from his unique perspective. The most heartwarming selection, "Baby Sister," reflects his pride in his new sibling and the love that is shared by the entire family.

Dance [17]

Written by Bill T. Jones and Susan Kuklin
Photographs by Susan Kuklin

Hardcover: Hyperion
Published 1998

Renowned dancer and choreographer Bill T. Jones is pictured in a great many dance poses demonstrating the expressiveness of the human body. This book has few words, but the color photographs of the talented artist speak volumes.

Daniel's Dog [18]

Written by Jo Ellen Bogart
Illustrated by Janet Wilson

Softcover: Blue Ribbon, Scholastic
Published 1990

Daniel is very understanding when his mother must spend less time with him and more with his new baby sister. It appears that Daniel is mature enough to play alone, until his mother learns that Daniel is playing with an imaginary dog—a ghost dog named Lucy. Daniel's belief in his special pet extends even further when he introduces his best friend, Norman, to another ghost dog.

Dave and the Tooth Fairy [19]

Written by Verna Allette Wilkins
Illustrated by Paul Hunt

Softcover: Tamarind
Published 1993

Dave sneezes, loosing a loose tooth in the process, but he cannot find it to give
to the tooth fairy. Amusingly, he substitutes his grandfather's dentures, plac-
ing them under his pillow. When the tooth fairy comes, she is shocked and
unable to afford the complete set of teeth that she finds. So, she returns to
Tooth Fairy Land to get extra money. By the time she returns, Grandfather
has found the missing tooth and put everything in its proper place, totally
bewildering the conscientious tooth fairy.

Dexter Gets Dressed! [20]

Written and illustrated by Ken Wilson-Max

Hardcover: Kingfisher
Published 1998

Young readers can help Dexter get dressed in this interactive book. Large type
and colorful illustrations reveal Dexter in various states of dress, and in felt
clothes that require a certain level of dexterity to manipulate the buttons,
zipper, and laces.

Oliver Strong, age 4

"One of my favorite
books is *The Best Way
to Play*. I liked it when
the dad ate all of the
hot dogs!"

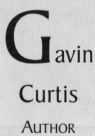

Gavin
Curtis
AUTHOR

"While there were not many books featuring children that looked like me when I was an emergent reader in the projects of the 1970s, it was the world of comic books that thoroughly empowered my literacy. They were inexpensive adventures written on a high-school level, and although at the time there were only a few black superheroes, it didn't seem to matter much. . . . It was, after all, as much of an imaginative leap for my white friends to identify with the adventures of an alien from Krypton as it was for me. It's one of the facts I try not to lose sight of when I create my books today."

OUR FAVORITE FROM
GAVIN CURTIS
The Bat Boy and His Violin [91]

Digby [21]

Written by Barbara Shook Hazen
Illustrated by Barbara Phillips-Duke

Softcover: HarperTrophy, HarperCollins
Published 1997

A young boy is eager to play with his dog, Digby, but Digby can't run and play anymore. The boy's sister explains that Digby is getting old and isn't as energetic as he once was. But Digby is still a good and loyal friend, and still very capable of giving lots of love. Colorfully illustrated, this book, one of the I Can Read series, offers an excellent lesson for young pet owners.

Emeka's Gift: An African Counting Story [22]

Written and photographed by Ifeoma Onyefulu

Hardcover: Cobblehill, Penguin USA
Published 1995

Captivating full-color photographs of the people of a village in southern Nigeria illustrate this counting story. *One* young Emeka is on his way to the next village to see his grandmother. Along the way he stops to find a gift for her. He considers *six* beautiful colored beads and *seven* musical instruments. Educational sidebars offer more detail about the interesting African curios. Companion titles include *A Is for Africa, Chidi Only Likes Blue: An African Book of Colors* [13], *Grandfather's Work: A Traditional Healer in Nigeria* [35], and *Ogbo: Sharing Life in an African Village.*

Everett Anderson's Friend [23]

Written by Lucille Clifton
Illustrated by Ann Grifalconi

Hardcover: Henry Holt
Published 1976

"*A girl named Maria who wins at ball is fun to play with after all.*"

Young Everett looks forward to meeting his new neighbors. He hopes that they have boys so he can have some new playmates, but is immediately deflated when he discovers that the family has only girls. Everett has no expectation that Maria and her sisters can play ball or shoot marbles until she proves otherwise. Poetic text is the hallmark of this series, which also includes *Everett Anderson's Christmas Coming, Everett Anderson's 1-2-3* [25], *Everett Anderson's Nine Month Long* [24], *Everett Anderson's Year* [26], and *Some of the Days of Everett Anderson* [77].

Everett Anderson's Nine Month Long [24]

Written by Lucille Clifton
Illustrated by Ann Grifalconi

Hardcover: Henry Holt
Published 1978

Young Everett is ambivalent about his mother's new marriage and the "almost" dad in his life. As the newlyweds plan for a new baby, they offer Everett assurances that he is still loved and cherished by his mother and accepted by his new stepfather. Their perceptive approach and Everett's tender reactions are offered in verse, as are other sensitive topics in the series, including *Everett Anderson's Christmas Coming, Everett Anderson's 1-2-3* [25], *Everett Anderson's Friend* [23], *Everett Anderson's Year* [26], and *Some of the Days of Everett Anderson* [77].

Everett Anderson's 1-2-3 [25]

Written by Lucille Clifton
Illustrated by Ann Grifalconi

Hardcover: Henry Holt
Published 1977

When Everett Anderson's mother announces that she plans to remarry, the young boy ponders the merits of being alone, being a family of two with his mother, and being a family of three with his mother and her new husband. Alone, he can eat a candy bar or play a drum. When there are two, he isn't lonely and has company for dinner. But three hardly seems necessary. A little talk with his mother's fiancé convinces Everett that three might be all right. Other books about Everett include *Everett Anderson's Christmas Coming, Everett Anderson's Friend* [23], *Everett Anderson's Nine Month Long* [24], *Everett Anderson's Year* [26], and *Some of the Days of Everett Anderson* [77].

Everett Anderson's Year [26]

Written by Lucille Clifton
Illustrated by Ann Grifalconi

Hardcover: Henry Holt
Published 1974

Seven-year-old Everett Anderson shares his reflections of each month of the year in twelve verses. Everett's unique perspective, as the only child of a single mother, are sometimes serious, sometimes emotional, and sometimes humorous. In September, Everett recites that he knows where Africa is, can count to ten, and went to school every day the previous year, so he wonders why he has to go again. This series also includes *Everett Anderson's Christmas Coming, Everett Anderson's 1-2-3* [25], *Everett Anderson's Friend* [23], *Everett Anderson's Nine Month Long* [24], and *Some of the Days of Everett Anderson* [77].

Father and Son [27]

Written by Denize Lauture
Illustrated by Jonathan Green

Softcover: Paperstar, Putnam
Published 1993

"*Down the road in the sun, Father and son hand in hand.*"

A father and son share special moments in this book, illustrated with richly colored paintings of their activities on a Sea Island beach. A short poem describes their time together—spent horseback riding, boating, walking, and reading.

From My Window [28]

Written by Olive Wong
Illustrated by Anna Rich

Hardcover: Silver
Published 1995

This brightly illustrated book of very few words features a thoughtful young boy peering out of his window. He watches the neighborhood activities until he is inspired to go outside to join in the wintertime play.

Furaha Means Happy!: A Book of Swahili Words [29]

Written and illustrated by Ken Wilson-Max

Hardcover: Hyperion
Published 2000

Moses and Wambui live in Kenya and speak the rhythmic Swahili language. In this bright picture book, they introduce young readers to the sounds of their native language. The story is written in English, but a number of common objects are identified with a picture and the English and Swahili words for children to learn. A companion book, *Halala Means Welcome!: A Book of Zulu Words* [36], is also available.

Get the Ball, Slim [30]

Written by Marcia Leonard
Illustrated by Dorothy Handelman

Softcover: Scholastic
Published 1998

Tim and Jim are identical twins in this story featuring only simple words for new readers. The brothers play with their dog, Slim, in a series of photographic illustrations. The simple nature of the text is reminiscent of the "Dick and Jane" books for primary students.

Getting Dressed [31]

Written by Dessie Moore
Illustrated by Chevelle Moore

Board Book: HarperFestival, HarperCollins
Published 1994

A little boy tells how he gets dressed in the morning with the help of his loving mother. Rich chalk colors are used to create the vibrant illustrations and the Afrocentric designs that border each page, making this simple book eye-catching to young readers. A companion book is *Let's Pretend*.

Golden Bear [32]

Written by Ruth Young
Illustrated by Rachel Isadora

Hardcover: Penguin USA
Published 1992

A cherubic toddler and his best friend, a golden teddy bear, are constant companions throughout the day. They do everything together, starting the day cuddling in a rocking chair and ending it by being tucked into bed side by side.

"*Dreaming dreamy dreams at night/ Golden Bear tucked in tight.*"

Good Night Baby [33]

Written by Cheryl Willis Hudson
Illustrated by George Ford

Board Book: Cartwheel, Scholastic
Published 1992

A busy baby, exhausted from his active day, prepares for bedtime with a comforting bath and a bedtime story before being tucked in by his loving mom. Companion books include *Animal Sounds for Baby* [1], *Good Morning Baby,* and *Let's Count Baby.*

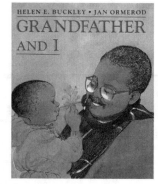

Grandfather and I [34]

Written by Helen E. Buckley
Illustrated by Jan Ormerod

Hardcover: Lothrop, Lee & Shepard, William Morrow
Published 1994

A preschool boy finds that all the people that he loves move too fast! His mom and dad are always in a hurry and his brother and sister are constantly in a rush. Grandfather, though, always seems to have time to walk with, talk with, and enjoy the company of the youngest member of the family. This is a touching story about the special bond that can exist between child and grandfather. A companion title is *Grandmother and I.*

Grandfather's Work: A Traditional Healer in Nigeria [35]

Written and photographed by Ifeoma Onyefulu

Hardcover: Millbrook
Published 1998

A young Nigerian boy introduces young readers to his mother, a baker; his uncle, an attorney; his aunt, a pot maker; and other family members with proud professions. The boy is most interested in his grandfather, a traditional healer, who uses his knowledge of plants and herbs to work medical magic in the lives of his patients. The young boy shares his grandfather's commitment to healing and vows to learn the art and carry on the tradition. Four other books in the same style and format are *A Is for Africa, Chidi Only Likes Blue: An African Book of Colors* [13], *Emeka's Gift: An African Counting Story* [22], and *Ogbo: Sharing Life in an African Village.*

Halala Means Welcome!: A Book of Zulu Words [36]

Written and illustrated by Ken Wilson-Max

Hardcover: Hyperion Books for Children
Published 1998

Bold, bright illustrations picture Michael and Chidi, two South African boys, who speak the musical Zulu language. Young readers can learn the Zulu words for friend, bus, milk, and twenty-two other everyday words, which are pictured on the oversized pages. A glossary and pronunciation guide are included in the back of the book. A companion book, *Furaha Means Happy!: A Book of Swahili Words* [29], is also available.

Halloween Monster [37]

Written and illustrated by Catherine Stock

Hardcover and softcover: Macmillan
Published 1990

Tommy participates in all the fun of the autumn season—playing in the raked leaves, sipping cider, and carving Halloween pumpkins—in this easy-to-read book. As the time for Halloween trick-or-treating draws nearer, Tommy admits to his mother that he is afraid of the ghosts, goblins, and monsters and declares that he wants to stay home. Mom reassures Tommy, allowing him to enjoy this childhood pleasure.

Hanging Out with Mom [38]

Written by Sonia W. Black
Illustrated by George Ford

Softcover: Cartwheel, Scholastic
Published 2000

A young boy and his mom spend the best part of the day together—right after school, before dinner. The two walk to the park, where they bond through their very special time together. This Hello Reader, Level 2 book is written in rhyme and includes parenting notes to help you find enriching activities that correspond with the story.

Sharon Draper

AUTHOR

"**M**y favorite book in the fourth grade was *Caddie Woodlawn.* The heroine was spunky and brave—qualities I admired. I wish she could have been an African American character. Perhaps I'll write a story one day with a black heroine like Caddie.

"The books that are available now that I wish I had when I was a child are the wonderful picture books with the strong positive black images, done by wonderful artists who capture the spirit and imagination of a child."

OUR FAVORITES FROM
SHARON DRAPER

Ziggy and the Black Dinosaurs [349]

Ziggy and the Black Dinosaurs: Lost in the Tunnel of Time [350]

Honey Hunters [39]

Retold and illustrated by Francesca Martin

Hardcover: Candlewick
Published 1992

Once, all of the animals in the African bush lived together in peace and harmony, and they all loved honey. A little gray bird, known as the honey guide, was called upon by a little boy to help him find a sweet honeycomb. Soon a rooster, a bush cat, an antelope, a leopard, a zebra, a lion, and an elephant joined the honey-hunting procession, one by one. After a long search, the bird finally led the group to a tree where a honeycomb was found. The boy split the honeycomb into four pieces, to be shared among the animals. But greed prevailed, pitting one animal against the other. So that is why, even today, roosters and bush cats, antelopes and leopards, zebras and lions, and elephants and humans do not get along.

I Can Count [40]

Written by Denise Lewis Patrick ☆ 120
Illustrated by Fred Willingham

Board Book: Golden, Western
Published 1996

An endearing little boy counts his belongings as he plays happily with them. He has *one* horse to ride, and *two* maracas to shake, but he seems happiest hugging his *five* puppies. Four companion titles from the Essence Books for Children series include *Baby's Bedtime* [4], *Baby's Colors, No Diapers for Baby,* and *Peekaboo Baby.*

I Love My Family [41]

Written by Wade Hudson
Illustrated by Cal Massey

Softcover: Scholastic
Published 1993

In this positive, loving story about a family reunion, a young boy demonstrates pride in every member of the family from the oldest, Aunt Nell, who is almost one hundred years old, to the youngest, his baby cousin, Ahshon. The family eats, plays, and reminisces until it is time to part, knowing that there will be another reunion next year.

I Need a Lunch Box [42]

Written by Jeanette Caines
Illustrated by Pat Cummings

Softcover: Trophy, HarperCollins
Published 1988

A family prepares their first-grade daughter for the new school year by buying her school clothes and supplies, including a brand-new lunch box. Her younger brother also wants a lunch box, so badly that he dreams of getting a whole collection of lunch boxes—a different color for each day of the week. The story is illustrated with vivid paintings that work with the text to help children learn the colors and match them to the written color names.

Island Baby [43]

Written and illustrated by Holly Keller

Hardcover and softcover: William Morrow
Published 1992

Simon spends his summer vacation helping Pop at his bird hospital. When Simon finds an injured baby flamingo, he takes it in and nurses it back to health, considering the bird to be his own pet. When the time comes to set the bird free, Simon is filled with mixed emotions.

Jafta and the Wedding [44]

Written by Hugh Lewin   *Reading Rainbow* Review Book
Illustrated by Lisa Kopper

Hardcover: Carolrhoda
Published 1983

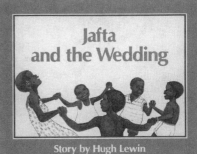

Young Jafta, a South African boy, enjoys the week-long celebration of his sister's wedding. Jafta and his friends watch with great interest as the wedding feast is prepared, the bride is readied, the young couple is married, and the celebration begins. The next day Jafta is reflective about his sister's new status as a married woman, but happy to have a new brother. The Jafta series includes four other titles: *Jafta, Jafta's Father, Jafta's Mother* [46], and *Jafta: The Town* [45].

Jafta: The Town [45]

Written by Hugh Lewin
Illustrated by Lisa Kopper

Reading Rainbow Review Book

Hardcover: Carolrhoda
Published 1984

Jafta is ambivalent about his visit to the city when he and his mother journey there to attend a funeral. While Jafta is happy to visit his father, who lives and works in the city, he is overwhelmed by the urban chaos. Jafta enjoys attending a soccer match and playing with new city friends but is repelled by the sights and smells of his father's factory job. Despite it all, when it is time to leave Jafta is saddened because his father cannot return with him and his mother to their village home. The Jafta series includes *Jafta, Jafta and the Wedding* [44], *Jafta's Mother* [46], and *Jafta's Father.*

Jafta's Mother [46]

Written by Hugh Lewin
Illustrated by Lisa Kopper

Reading Rainbow Review Book

Hardcover: Carolrhoda
Published 1983

Jafta, a young South African boy, offers a loving tribute to his mother by recounting her many wonderful characteristics. She is, he says, "like the earth—full of goodness," and "like the sky, she's always there." Jafta's love and esteem for his mother, which she returns in kind, abound in this sentimental book. The Jafta series includes *Jafta, Jafta and the Wedding* [44], *Jafta's Father,* and *Jafta: The Town* [45].

Jake and Honeybunch Go to Heaven [47]

Written and illustrated by Margot Zemach

Hardcover: Farrar Straus & Giroux
Published 1982

In this retelling of an African American folktale, Jake and his mule, Honeybunch, were sent straight to heaven after the stubborn mule stalled on the tracks in the way of an oncoming train. The two bypassed St. Peter and went right on in through the Pearly Gates. Jake helped himself to a pair of wings and flew recklessly throughout heaven. Honeybunch kicked and carried on until the other angels scattered in every direction. God was about to banish the two from heaven forever but decided to give them a chance to redeem themselves, assigning them the job of hanging the moon and stars every night and taking them down every morning. And to this day, Jake and Honeybunch keep their place in heaven because they do such a fine job.

Jamal's Busy Day [48]

Written by Wade Hudson
Illustrated by George Ford

Hardcover and softcover: Just Us
Published 1991

Jamal understands the importance of his job as a student and his role as a family member, based on the positive role modeling of his parents. Every day, he prepares for his job of learning by washing up and brushing his teeth. He works hard at school, drawing pictures, doing math, and helping the teacher. Of course, the commute home is not easy, since the school bus is always so crowded! When he finally gets home, he does his homework, sets the table, and spends time with his family.

Joe Can Count [49]

Written and illustrated by Jan Ormerod

Softcover: Mulberry, William Morrow
Published 1986

Joe, a typical little boy, demonstrates that he can count from one to ten by numbering a series of fish, frogs, mice, chicks, turtles, snails, spiders, ants, sheep, and pigs. As he counts each group, young readers will see a picture representation of the number as well as the numerals to help them understand the correlation between the number of objects and the numeric symbol.

Jonathan and His Mommy [50]

Written by Irene Smalls ☆ 160
Illustrated by Michael Hays

Hardcover and softcover: Little, Brown
Published 1992

Jonathan and his mommy take a walk, a skip, a jump, a dance, and a run through the neighborhood, enjoying each other's company. This popular book exemplifies the love and affection shared between a mother and her child.

Joshua by the Sea [51]

Written by Angela Johnson ☆ 64
Illustrated by Rhonda Mitchell

Board Book: Orchard
Published 1994

Little Joshua enjoys a special day on the beach along with his loving parents and attentive big sister. The illustrations show him enjoying the sun, sand, and sea. A gentle poem describes his special day. Other books about young Joshua are *Mama Bird, Baby Birds* [54]; *Joshua's Night Whispers* [52]; and *Rain Feet.*

Joshua's Night Whispers [52]

Written by Angela Johnson ☆ 64
Illustrated by Rhonda Mitchell

Board Book: Orchard
Published 1994

From his bed, young Joshua tunes in to the sounds of the night. The scary night whispers compel him to leave his room and walk down the hall to the comforting arms of his daddy, who holds him warm and safe. Three other books, *Mama Bird, Baby Birds* [54]; *Joshua by the Sea* [51]; and *Rain Feet,* are also about the adventurous young Joshua.

Kofi and the Butterflies [53]

Written by Sandra Horn
Illustrated by Lynne Wiley

Softcover: Africa World
Published 1995

Kofi loves butterflies and spends hours watching their graceful flights through the park. One day, after saving a butterfly from the net of another boy, Kofi gets an extraordinary reward—the butterfly lights on his shoulder and invites him into the secret kingdom of the butterflies. Kofi is magically swept into the inner world, where he is surrounded by millions of the beautiful creatures. And then, just as suddenly, Kofi is returned to the park, and realizes that he must have had a fantastic dream . . . or did he?

Mama Bird, Baby Birds [54]

Written by Angela Johnson ☆ 64
Illustrated by Rhonda Mitchell

Board Book: Orchard
Published 1994

Young Joshua and his sister find a nest of baby birds in their yard. As they watch the mother bird feed and tend her young, they are reminded of their own loving mother. Three other books, *Joshua by the Sea* [51], *Joshua's Night Whispers* [52], and *Rain Feet,* follow the adventures of this young boy.

Max [55]

Written and illustrated by Ken Wilson-Max

Board Book: Hyperion
Published 1998

A little boy named Max plays with his pet pig in twelve colorfully illustrated pages. The bright, simple art will attract young readers, as will the manipulative tabs, wheels, and flaps designed for busy little hands. Other interactive books about the busy boy are *Max Loves Sunflowers* [56], *Max's Letter* [57], and *Max's Money* [58].

Max Loves Sunflowers [56]

Written and illustrated by Ken Wilson-Max

Board Book: Hyperion
Published 1998

Max, a cute round-faced boy, decides to plant a flower garden. Each step is pictured in large block illustrations with a series of manipulative pop-ups, flaps, and tabs that allow young readers to join in the fun. Three other books make up a collection of books about this character: *Max* [55], *Max's Letter* [57], and *Max's Money* [58].

Max's Letter [57]

Written and illustrated by Ken Wilson-Max

Board Book: Jump at the Sun, Hyperion
Published 1999

Young children will be amused by and spend hours with this interactive book. In the inside cover, they will discover a bag stuffed with a removable cardboard letter. In the following brightly colored pages they will find slotted boxes, bags, and mailboxes in which to deliver and redeliver their letter. Other titles about this character include *Max* [55], *Max Loves Sunflowers* [56], and *Max's Money* [58].

Max's Money [58]

Written and illustrated by Ken Wilson-Max

Board Book: Jump at the Sun, Hyperion
Published 1999

Little children will love this engaging interactive book. Each page features a pocket or a slot in the phone, wallet, bank, or bubble gum machine that will accept the cardboard coin that comes in the book. Other titles about this character include *Max* [55], *Max Loves Sunflowers* [56], and *Max's Letter* [57].

Me and My Family Tree [59]

Written by Carole Boston Weatherford
Illustrated by Michelle Mills

Board Book: Black Butterfly, Writers & Readers
Published 1997

A little boy compares his facial features to those of his family in this rhyming verse. He has his brother's chin, his mother's hair, and his father's mouth, all illustrated in sensitive pictures of the child and those he loves. Other titles in this series dealing with self-esteem topics include *Mighty Menfolk* [60], *My Favorite Toy, My Hair Is Beautiful . . .Because It's Mine!, My Skin Is Brown,* and *Grandma and Me.*

Mighty Menfolk [60]

Written by Carole Boston Weatherford
Illustrated by Michelle Mills

Board Book: Black Butterfly, Writers & Readers
Published 1997

A young boy recognizes strength and character in all of the men who surround him. In rhythmic verse, he identifies business neighbors, like the barber and storekeeper; service workers, like the policemen and firemen; and family members, like his uncle, father, and grandfather, who influence his life and set fine examples for him. Other books in this series about positive self-images include *Grandma and Me, Me and My Family Tree* [59], *My Favorite Toy, My Hair Is Beautiful . . . Because It's Mine!,* and *My Skin Is Brown.*

My Best Friend [61]

Written by P. Mignon Hinds ☆ 58
Illustrated by Cornelius Van Wright

Hardcover: Golden, Western
Published 1997

A young boy demonstrates a perfect understanding of the nature of relationships as he complains about all the things he does not like about his friend Omar: Omar broke his favorite model airplane, and always takes the window seat on the bus. On the other hand, he later recalls the special things that still make Omar his best friend: Omar shares his baseball cards and peanut butter cookies, and he tells funny jokes. This title, and its companion books, *I Like Me* and *What I Want to Be,* are positive self-image stories in the Essence Books for Children series.

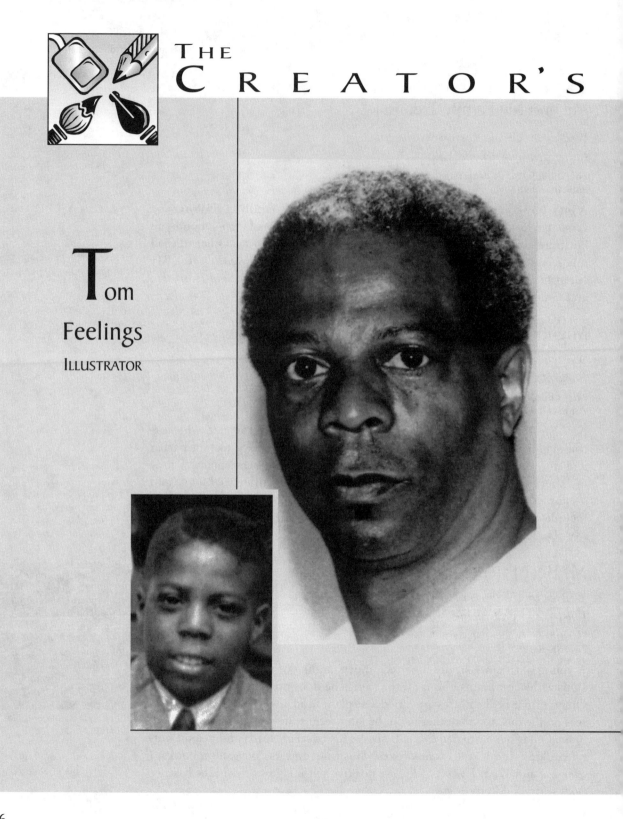

Tom
Feelings
ILLUSTRATOR

REFLECTIONS

"**W**hen I was very young, I enjoyed reading all kinds of fairy tales, including the world of fantasy. Later on I enjoyed adventure books based on historical situations, like *The Three Musketeers, The Man in the Iron Mask,* and *Robin Hood,* but especially those stories that were seen through the eyes of a child or young person, like *Treasure Island* or *Jungle Book*. Of course, if all of those books had been written with black characters I could have really gotten into them and lived through them.

"I know this is the main reason as a young adult in art school that I created the comic strip *Tommy Traveler: In the World of Negro History,* using myself as the model of a young boy transformed back into black history retelling and reliving that past, but this time through and with black heroes and heroines, finally hooking together, in the form of comic strip (and years later black children's books), my early interest in fantasy and realism.

"Recently I picked up a self-published book, *Grandpa, Is Everything Black Bad?* by Lynn Holman. In the introduction, Dr. Wade Nobles writes, 'This is a story all parents should read to their children, because it points out clearly that self love is the most precious gift and that as black people we have a glorious heritage that runs through our veins.' I would have loved to have read that at an early age, and been strengthened by it."

OUR FAVORITES FROM
TOM FEELINGS

Tommy Traveler in the World of Black History [240]

Zamani Goes to Market [260]

My Mama Needs Me [62]

Written by Mildred Pitts Walter ☆ 174
Illustrated by Pat Cummings

Hardcover: Lothrop, Lee & Shepard
Published 1983

Sweet little Jason is so excited and feels so responsible when his mother brings his new baby sister home from the hospital that he sits steadfastly at home, knowing that his mama will need his help. As he sits and waits, all his mama and sister do is sleep . . . and sleep . . . and sleep. Still, he waits, knowing that at any moment he will be called upon to help. When Mama finally wakes up, she warmly acknowledges her son's devotion and then relieves him of his tough, self-imposed duty.

Noah [63]

Written by Patricia L. Gauch
Illustrated by Jonathan Green

Hardcover: Philomel, Putnam
Published 1994

The well-known Bible story of Noah and the ark is told in this colorful picture book. The illustrations of the menagerie of animals are vibrant and eye-catching, but the intriguing feature is that Noah and his family are illustrated in the multiple colors of the black race.

Oh, No, Toto! [64]

Written by Katrin Hyman Tchana and Louise Tchana Pami
Illustrated by Colin Bootman

Hardcover: Scholastic
Published 1997

Little Toto is a handful for his grandmother, Big Mimi, who takes him to shop in her West African marketplace. Toto's appetite is greater than his reach. First he spills a tray of puffpuffs while reaching for the biggest one. Then he upsets an entire tray of hard-boiled eggs while diving for one. Finally, Toto takes a fall right into a tub of palm oil while trying to reach a banana! The exuberant two-year-old's mischief is complete when he rolls in the sand and becomes the muddiest child in the village.

On the Day I Was Born [65]

Written by Debbi Chocolate
Illustrated by Melodye Rosales

Hardcover: Scholastic
Published 1995

A baby boy is born to a family that celebrates a beautiful tradition. The new baby is held up to the full moon's light by his father, and his dedicated relatives surround him to welcome him to the family. This book is so touching that every new parent will want one as a keepsake for the new baby. The illustrations are so vivid and three-dimensional that they look like photographs.

Palampam Day [66]

Written by David and Phillis Gershator
Illustrated by Enrique O. Sanchez

Hardcover: Marshall Cavendish
Published 1997

In this whimsical story, young Turo is hungry but can't get anything to eat and drink. The coconuts in the tree chide him not to eat them, the frog in the barrel scolds him for dipping into the water, and the sweet potatoes turn him away when he tries to dig them up. Turo consults Papa Tata Wanga to try to understand why all the foods are talking. The mysterious event is explained as Palampam Day, "the day all things find their voice and say whatever they feel like saying." Papa Tata Wanga assures Turo that this strange event happens very rarely—only once in a blue moon. Turo goes to bed to wait for the new day, when everything will return to normal.

Peter's Chair [67]

Written and illustrated by Ezra Jack Keats   ***Reading Rainbow* Review Book**

Softcover: Puffin, Penguin Putnam
Published 1967

Peter becomes concerned when his parents begin to pass all of his things on to his new baby sister. First they paint his cradle pink, and then his high chair and crib. When they begin eyeing his special chair, Peter takes the chair to his room for safekeeping. As he sits on the chair, pondering the situation, he reaches the mature conclusion that he is too big for the chair, and that he should pass it on to the new baby. Other books about Peter include *Goggles, Letter to Amy, Pet Show, The Snowy Day* [76], and *Whistle for Willie.*

Pretty Brown Face [68]

Written by Andrea Davis Pinkney
Illustrated by Brian Pinkney

Board Book: Red Wagon, Harcourt Brace
Published 1997

A toddler sees his reflection in a mirror and studies his own image. He looks at the eyes, nose, lips, and hair on his pretty brown face while his proud father watches. A mirrored page at the end will allow little readers to admire their own beautiful faces. Other board books by the same husband-and-wife creators are *I Smell Honey; Shake, Shake, Shake;* and *Watch Me Dance.*

Robo's Favorite Places [69]

Written by Wade Hudson
Illustrated by Cathy Johnson

Softcover: Just Us
Published 1999

Robo's imagination runs wild when his teacher asks the class to tell about their favorite places. Robo considers his favorites—the skating rink, the neighborhood playhouse, the swimming pool. Then Robo remembers that his favorite place in the world is sitting at his computer working on the World Wide Web, which can take him anyplace in the world.

Rumplestiltskin [70]

Written by Naomi Fox
Illustrated by Neal Fox

Softcover and audiotape: Confetti
Published 1993

The traditional fairy tale is told again in this colorful book/audiotape set. Young readers can read along as they hear the well-known story told in the richly textured voice of actor Robert Guillaume. The Confetti Company series of fairy tales also includes *A Christmas Carol, A Different Kind of Christmas, The Frog Prince, Hansel and Gretel, The Shoemaker and the Elves,* and *Sleeping Beauty.*

Sam [71]

Written by Ann Herbert Scott
Illustrated by Symeon Shimin

Hardcover: McGraw Hill
Published 1967

Sam becomes more and more depressed as, one by one, his family members reject him. First his mother sends him away because she is too busy in the kitchen. Then his big brother shoos him away because he is studying. His sister screams at him for playing with her doll. Finally, his father sends him away because he is too busy with his work. When Sam begins to cry, everyone realizes what they have done, and they stop to offer him the attention that he deserves.

Sharing Danny's Dad [72]

Written by Angela Shelf Medearis
Illustrated by Jan Spivey Gilchrist

Hardcover: Good Year, HarperCollins
Published 1995

His own daddy had to work today, but thank goodness his friend Danny is willing to share his dad for the day. Danny's dad generously tickles, plays ball with, and pushes both boys on the swing in this story of sharing.

She Come Bringing Me That Little Baby Girl [73]

Written by Eloise Greenfield ☆ 42
Illustrated by John Steptoe

Softcover: Trophy, HarperCollins
Published 1974

Kevin is prepared for a new baby brother, but to his surprise the new baby is a girl! To make matters worse, everybody's attention is turned to the baby, making Kevin feel left out. A conversation with his mother helps Kevin understand that he is still loved and that there is a special new role for him as a big brother. ***Nonstandard English.***

Eloise Greenfield

AUTHOR

"For someone who spent so much of her childhood reading, it is strange that I remember very little of the content of the books I read. I remember loving language, and I remember the wonderful feeling of being caught up in a story, but titles, plots, and characters have long been forgotten. Maybe some part of the emotional connection was missing. Maybe if some of the stories and poems had been about me . . ."

OUR FAVORITES FROM
ELOISE GREENFIELD

First Pink Light [127]

For the Love of the Game: Michael Jordan and Me [128]

She Come Bringing Me That Little Baby Girl [73]

Water, Water [81]

William and the Good Old Days [253]

Dudley Williams, age 9

"I think that *My Best Friend* is very good because even though Omar breaks his friend's model airplane, they still stay friends."

Simeon's Sandbox [74]

Written by Keith Suranna
Illustrated by Lauren Attinello

Board Book: Little Simon, Simon & Schuster
Published 1997

Baby Simeon, of the *Gullah Gullah Island* television series, is featured in this book about his sandbox adventures. Simeon spends the entire day imaginatively creating a sand castle and mud pies. A companion book is *Binyah Binyah's Big Backyard.*

Snow on Snow on Snow [75]

Written by Cheryl Chapman
Illustrated by Synthia Saint James ☆ 146

Hardcover: Dial, Penguin USA
Published 1994

Bold, block-style paintings illustrate the story of a young boy's day playing in the snow. The brief, simple text includes repetitive word sequences to reinforce the action of this wintertime story.

The Snowy Day [76]

Written and illustrated by Ezra Jack Keats

Caldecott Award
Reading Rainbow Review Book

Hardcover and softcover: Viking, Penguin
Published 1962

Upon awakening, young Peter finds a yard full of fresh new snow. Outside, bundled in his snowsuit, he makes tracks and snow angels, sleds, and enjoys his wonderful winter playground. Other titles in the series about the playful Peter include *Goggles, Letter to Amy, Pet Show, Peter's Chair* [67], and *Whistle for Willie.*

Some of the Days of Everett Anderson [77]

Written by Lucille Clifton
Illustrated by Evaline Ness

Hardcover: Henry Holt
Published 1970

Young readers will be entertained by these brief poems about six-year-old Everett Anderson's view of everyday events that happen during his Monday morning, Tuesday all day, Saturday night, and other times. They may relate to his joy of being a six-year-old boy, his preference for getting wet rather than using an umbrella, or how he misses his daddy most on Sunday mornings. Other books about Everett Anderson include *Everett Anderson's 1-2-3* [25], *Everett Anderson's Christmas Coming, Everett Anderson's Friend* [23], *Everett Anderson's Nine Month Long* [24], and *Everett Anderson's Year* [26].

Something Special [78]

Written by Nicola Moon
Illustrated by Alex Ayliffe

Hardcover: Peachtree
Published 1997

Charlie is frustrated and a little angry with his mother, who is too busy with the new baby to help him find something to take to school for show-and-tell. In fact, Mom puts him off for several days in a row because the baby always needs her attention. Charlie is desperate to find a unique item to take to school until he realizes the answer is right under his nose. Charlie takes his baby sister to show-and-tell and is met with enthusiasm for his one-of-a-kind presentation! Primary-color collages embellish this simple story.

Tukama Tootles the Flute: A Tale from the Antilles [79]

Retold by Phillis Gershator
Illustrated by Synthia Saint James ☆ 146

Hardcover: Orchard
Published 1994

> " *When the giant went out in the morning to catch fish and collect prickly pears and jumbie beads, he told his wife, 'Give that boy a lot of johnnycake today. Fatten him up good, and we'll eat him for supper.' "*

Tukama is a naughty child who ignores his chores in this Caribbean version of "Jack and the Beanstalk." Despite his grandmother's constant admonitions, he runs off to a forbidden place. He gets captured by a two-headed giant and his wife, who intend to fatten Tukama up to eat for supper. In a suspenseful climax, Tukama uses his wits and engages the giant's wife with his tootling flute until he is able to escape.

Uh-oh! It's Mama's Birthday! [80]

Written by Naturi Thomas
Illustrated by Keinyo White

Hardcover: Albert Whitman
Published 1997

Jason's heart is in the right place as he goes out with his only dollar to buy a birthday present for his mama. His first choice, a dress, is too expensive, so he uses seventy-five cents to buy her some jelly bears. In an amusing sequence, Jason slowly eats the jelly bears, one color at a time, rationalizing that she does not like the green ones . . . the red ones . . . the yellow ones . . . until they are all gone! Remorsefully, Jason buys Mama a balloon with his last quarter, but accidentally loses it. He returns home, disheartened, only to find out that all Mama really wants is a hug.

Water, Water [81]

Written by Eloise Greenfield ☆ 42
Illustrated by Jan Spivey Gilchrist

Hardcover: HarperFestival, HarperCollins
Published 1999

A young boy takes inventory of all the places where he finds water, from his fishbowl and drinking cup to streams, lakes, and fountains. Keep up the fun by challenging your young reader to add to this watery list.

When I Am Old with You [82]

Written by Angela Johnson ☆ 64   **Coretta Scott King Honor: Author**
Illustrated by David Soman

Hardcover and softcover: Orchard, Franklin Watts
Published 1990

A young boy demonstrates his love and commitment to his elderly grandfather when he lists all of the quiet activities that he is willing to do with his grandfather, including sitting in the rocking chair, swatting flies, and playing cards under a shade tree. Affectionate pictures of the two companions accompany the child's warm sentiments.

When Will Sarah Come? [83]

Written by Elizabeth Fitzgerald Howard
Photographed by Nina Crews

Hardcover: Greenwillow
Published 1999

Sarah is off to school for the first time, but her little brother is left home to await her return. Photographic illustrations show the young preschooler playing with his toys as he patiently waits. But every time he hears a noise outside, he anxiously runs to the door to see if it is Sarah. When Sarah finally arrives, he is happy to have his playmate back at home.

Will There Be a Lap for Me? [84]

Written by Dorothy Corey
Illustrated by Nancy Poydar

Hardcover and softcover: Albert Whitman
Published 1992

Kyle's favorite place is his mommy's lap, but as a new baby grows inside her, his special place disappears more and more each week. Then the baby comes and is always in Mom's arms, again blocking his way to her lap. At last Mom makes special time for Kyle and returns him to the warmth and comfort of the lap he loves. Many small children have had or will have this experience and can be assured of Mommy's unwavering love, despite any new babies.

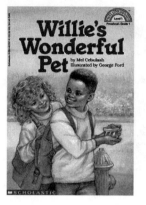

Willie's Wonderful Pet [85]

Written by Mel Cebulash
Illustrated by George Ford

Softcover: Cartwheel, Scholastic
Published 1993

Willie takes his pet to school for show-and-tell. The other children bring their dogs, birds, fish, and rabbits, but Willie brings something entirely different— a pet worm, in a paper cup filled with dirt. Nobody realizes what a worm can do until Willie gives them a demonstration of the worm's special talent.

Books for Early Readers

I**N OUR EXPERIENCE**, both as mothers and as book sellers, a boy in the elementary age group would much rather read a book about a male character than about a female character. His loyal association as a male is validated by choosing books about boys doing "guy" things. And that is perfectly okay.

But in this day and age there is nothing wrong with broadening his view of what both boys and girls can do—in essence challenging traditional gender roles. The boys and men of today are certainly socialized to be strong, fearless, sporty, adventurous, and in command, but they are also more free to be intellectual, sensitive, helpful, and artistic.

It is especially important for African American boys to embrace a wide spectrum of attributes to help them be more successful in twenty-first-century society. That is why the books we present to boys should be carefully selected to help counteract both the traditional gender bias that hinders both males and females from developing as a whole person and the notion that African Americans are somehow different from or inferior to others.

We have included 175 positive selections for and about boys and men in this section. The diverse selection gives young boys the opportunity to see themselves more expansively.

There are profiles of strong African American men achieving, accomplishing, and contributing in the many wonderful biographical books and books of historical fiction, such as *Coming Home: From the Life of Langston Hughes* [114]; *Dear Benjamin Banneker* [119]; and a fictionalized story about Booker T. Washington, *More Than Anything Else* [186]. These characters embody the strength of will, courage, and determination that we would all hope for young men.

A number of books present young boys learning important life virtues, such as honesty and integrity. Take the young boy who struggles between right and wrong in *Bimmi Finds a Cat* [100], or the boy who must rebuild trust with his grandmother after a personal indiscretion in *Keepers* [162]. We are also pleased to share several titles that demonstrate an appreciation for education and achievement, such as *The Barber's Cutting Edge* [90] and *Be Patient, Abdul* [92].

Of course, boys will be boys and we wouldn't have it any other way, so they will love several high-spirited books like *Christopher, Please Clean Up Your Room!* [112] and *Clean Your Room, Harvey Moon!* [113], about stereotypically untidy boys, or *Little Muddy Waters: A Gullah Folk Tale* [173] and *Little Eight John* [172], stories about naughty boys who get their comeuppance, and *The Boy and the Ghost* [105] and *The Adventures of Sparrowboy* [86], about brave, risk-taking boys.

There are also several books that are supportive of a young boy's self-image as an African American, such as *The Black Snowman* [103], *An Angel Just Like Me* [88], and *Grandpa, Is Everything Black Bad?* [136], which are all extraordinary reinforcements of racial dignity.

Of course, you can't always count on your young reader to get the message. While it may be clear to you that he is reading about wonderful, strong, well-rounded, confident boys and men, he may miss that point. So, take the time to discuss the storylines, the characters, and the situations with your young boy to make sure he gets the most from the reading experience.

The Adventures of Sparrowboy [86]

Written and illustrated by Brian Pinkney

Hardcover and softcover: Simon & Schuster
Published 1997

In this fun-loving fantasy, Henry the paper boy runs into a small sparrow while on his paper route. In the collision, Henry is magically transformed into a flying superhero, like his favorite comic-strip hero, Falconman. He can see everything from his airborne vantage point, so he is able to witness the town bully's mischief and put an end to it.

Alvin Ailey [87]

Written by Andrea Davis Pinkney   **Reading Rainbow** Review Book
Illustrated by Brian Pinkney

Hardcover and softcover: Hyperion
Published 1993

Choreographer Alvin Ailey blazed a path in modern dance by blending African American dance movements with traditional modern-dance techniques. This simply told biography tells of Ailey's inspiration to dance and how he established himself as a genius in the field. Ailey's contribution to the larger American dance culture can be a source of pride and encouragement for any African American child.

An Angel Just Like Me [88]

Written by Mary Hoffman
Illustrated by Cornelius Van Wright and Ying-Hwa Hu

Hardcover: Dial, Penguin USA
Published 1997

Young Tyler begins to ponder a problem as his family decorates their Christmas tree. Why do all the angel tree-toppers look like girls and why are none of them black? Tyler takes it upon himself to find a new angel for the family tree that looks like himself—a black boy. Tyler's search captures the need of children to see themselves reflected throughout their worlds. This touching and self-affirming story is beautifully illustrated.

Anansi Finds a Fool [89]

Written by Verna Aardema
Illustrated by Bryna Waldman

Hardcover: Dial
Published 1992

Vibrant illustrations and descriptive text tell the story of Anansi, a lazy man who is humorously outsmarted by his would-be friend, Bonsu. Anansi plans to find a fool to join him in a new fishing business. He imagines tricking the fool into doing all the hard work, while he takes all the fish. But the tables are turned in this African tale that perfectly demonstrates the moral of the story: "When you dig a hole for someone else, you will fall into it yourself."

The Barber's Cutting Edge [90]

Written by Gwendolyn Battle-Lavert
Illustrated by Raymond Holbert

Hardcover: Children's Book Press
Published 1994

While sitting in the barber's chair, Rashaad challenges his barber, Mr. Bigalow, to a vocabulary quiz, posing words like *abolish*, *idiosyncratic*, and *bewilderment*. Mr. Bigalow seems to have an excellent command of the words, defining each one perfectly. As Rashaad's admiration grows, Mr. Bigalow makes repeated trips to the back room, supposedly for a little more talcum powder, or to fix his hair clippers. When he disappears again, after the word *niche* is presented, Rashaad follows him and discovers Mr. Bigalow's cutting edge—a dictionary! Young readers will enjoy the artful illustrations, learn the definitions of some new words, and discover the power of a dictionary.

The Bat Boy and His Violin [91]

Written by Gavin Curtis ☆ 18
Illustrated by E. B. Lewis

Hardcover: Simon & Schuster
Published 1998

Young Reginald is a consummate musician who would rather play his violin than do anything else, much to his father's chagrin. His father, who manages the Dukes, a losing team in the Negro National Baseball League, decides to recruit Reginald as a bat boy for the team. Reginald is a disaster as a bat boy, but the team finds his violin music inspirational. As Reginald plays the music of Mozart, Beethoven, and Bach in the dugout during the games, the team begins to perform to new heights. Finally, the Dukes are in the position to win a pennant against the hottest team in the league. Win or lose, Reginald has made a difference, earning the respect of the team and the gratitude of his father.

Be Patient, Abdul [92]

Written and illustrated by Dolores Sandoval

Hardcover: Margaret K. McElderry, Simon & Schuster
Published 1996

Seven-year-old Abdul lives in Sierra Leone, where education cannot be taken for granted. School is not free, and children must work to help pay their own way. In this simply illustrated book, Abdul sells oranges, anxious to earn enough money to pay for school fees. Only after perseverance, hard work, patience, and the support of his parents is Abdul able to earn the money and return to school. Young readers should know that an education is a privilege that is not always available or free to all the children of the world.

Because You're Lucky [93]

Written by Irene Smalls ☆ 160
Illustrated by Michael Hays

Hardcover: Little, Brown
Published 1997

Kevin feels immediately at home when he comes to live with his aunt and her family. The young boy arrives at Aunt Laura's with nothing more than the clothes on his back. Aunt Laura immediately welcomes her nephew as a son, but her own son, Jonathan, is not so gracious. Jonathan isn't willing to share or to befriend his new roommate. But over time, the two bond and forge a brotherly relationship. Both Kevin and Jonathan come to understand how lucky they are to be blessed with family and each other.

The Bells of Christmas [94]

Written by Virginia Hamilton
Illustrated by Lambert Davis

Coretta Scott King Honor: Author

Softcover: Harcourt Brace
Published 1986

Twelve-year-old Jason Bell and his family celebrate a traditional midwestern Christmas in the winter of 1890 with a visit from Uncle Levi and his family. All of their wishes come true: it snows, unexpectedly, so they have a white Christmas; there are plenty of pleasing presents under the tree; the holiday meal is fantastic; and Uncle Levi brings a special gift for Papa. This is a beautiful story of family life in a simpler time, but with all the timeless magic of Christmas.

The Best Way to Play [95]

Written by Bill Cosby
Illustrated by Varnette P. Honeywood

Hardcover and softcover: Cartwheel, Scholastic
Published 1997

Little Bill and his friends are keen fans of the television show *Space Explorer,* so when Space Captain Zeke, the show's star, promotes a new video game based on the show, the friends all run home to ask their parents to buy it. Only Andrew is successful in getting a copy of the game, but he is happy to share it with his friends. It doesn't take long before the kids have mastered the game and are bored again. That's when they turn to an imaginative game, pretending that they are Space Explorers, and discover that their play is far more fun than the video game. Other books in the Little Bill series are: *The Day I Saw My Father Cry* [117], *The Day I Was Rich* [118], *The Meanest Thing to Say* [180], *Money Troubles* [184], *My Big Lie* [188], *One Dark and Scary Night* [206], *Shipwreck Sunday, Super-Fine Valentine* [237], *The Treasure Hunt* [241], and *The Worst Day of My Life* [257].

Big Jabe [96]

Written by Jerdine Nolen
Illustrated by Kadir Nelson

Hardcover: Lothrop, Lee & Shepard
Published 2000

A slave woman named Addy goes to the river to fish one day. But instead of catching fish, she finds a little boy, named Jabe, floating in a basket. She takes him home to raise as her own. Jabe, who is no ordinary child, grows by leaps and bounds until he is a giant of a man. Maybe it is only a coincidence, but from the day Jabe arrives everything on Plenty Plantation seems to grow and mature at unusual rates. And Jabe can outwork fifty other men. Perhaps it is another coincidence, but since Jabe came slaves began disappearing without a trace from Plenty Plantation. Some say that the gifted Jabe was sent to lift the burdens of others. Young readers may agree!

Bigmama's [97]

Written and illustrated by Donald Crews

Hardcover and softcover: Greenwillow
Published 1991

A grown man fondly reminisces about his family's annual trip to Cottondale, Florida, to visit Bigmama, his grandmother. She wasn't big; they called her Bigmama because she was their mama's mother. Visiting her farm was the highlight of his summers. Memories of playing on Bigmama's farm with his brothers and sisters and large family dinners are nostalgically presented. The sequel to this book is *Shortcut*.

Bill Pickett: Rodeo-Ridin' Cowboy [98]

Written by Andrea D. Pinkney
Illustrated by Brian Pinkney

Hardcover: Gulliver, Harcourt Brace
Published 1996

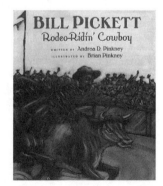

The story of Bill Pickett, the first African American to be inducted into the National Cowboy Hall of Fame, is told in this biographical story book. Bill, the son of ex-slaves, became a heralded rodeo star, largely because of his dramatic bulldogging (steer wrestling) style. Bill incapacitated the steer in this man-vs.-beast sport by actually biting into the animal's lip! Scratchboard illustrations accentuate this true story about one of the few African Americans in this daring sport.

Billy the Great [99]

Written by Rosa Guy
Illustrated by Caroline Binch

Hardcover: Delacorte
Published 1991

As young Billy grows, his proud parents are amazed by everything he does and continually speculate on his great future. Perhaps he will become a doctor, a professor, or even a great soccer player. But Billy is already a great person, which he demonstrates when he makes friends with his new neighbor, Rod. Billy's parents consider Rod and his parents to be unsuitable as friends because they are a blue-collar family, and white. Billy, however, accepts and appreciates Rod for the fine person he is, a setting an example of inclusion for his parents.

Bimmi Finds a Cat [100]

Written by Elisabeth J. Stewart
Illustrated by James E. Ransome

Hardcover: Clarion, Houghton Mifflin
Published 1996

Bimmi, a young Creole boy living on Galveston Island, is heartbroken when his beloved cat, Crabmeat, is found dead. The anguished boy finds another cat, but it obviously belongs to someone else. Bimmi is understandably torn between his desire for another pet to replace Crabmeat and finding the cat's rightful owner, which he ultimately does. His honesty is rewarded by the owner's considerate offer to share the cat. **Nonstandard English.**

Birthday [101]

Written and illustrated by John Steptoe

Softcover: Henry Holt
Published 1972

Javaka Shatu is celebrating his eighth birthday. Before his birth, Javaka's parents immigrated from America to the town of Yoruba, where they thought that as black people, they could live a better life. Family, neighbors, and friends are all coming to a party in celebration of the special occasion. Javaka feels so positive about his home and the fellowship his family shares with their neighbors that, for his birthday, he wishes they could all live together forever.

Black Cowboy, Wild Horses: A True Story [102]

Written by Julius Lester ☆ 80
Illustrated by Jerry Pinkney

Hardcover: Dial, Penguin Putnam
Published 1998

The legendary Bob Lemmons rode his way to cowboy fame as a former slave who could track wild horses better than anyone. In this true story, young readers will ride with Bob as he methodically tracks a herd of wild mustangs, then slowly and patiently integrates himself into the herd until they hardly notice him. When the time is right, Bob and his own horse, Warrior, challenge the lead stallion for control of the herd. That battle won, Bob and Warrior lead the unwitting herd to the corral as the astonished crowd cheers the accomplishment. Intense watercolor paintings accompany the story.

"Throughout that day and the next he rode with the horses. For Bob there was only the bulging of the horses' dark eyes, the quivering of their flesh, the rippling of muscles and bending of bones in their bodies. He was now sky and plains and grass and river and horse."

The Black Snowman [103]

Written by Phil Mendez
Illustrated by Carole Byard

Hardcover and softcover: Scholastic
Published 1989

Young Jacob, anguished by poverty and disgusted with his blackness, is reinvigorated by a surreal encounter with a mystic black snowman made of sooty snow. The snowman's magical kente cloth scarf reveals to Jacob visions of the great heritage of the black race and helps instill a sense of pride and personal strength that he had never known.

The Blue and the Gray [104]

Written by Eve Bunting
Illustrated by Ned Bittinger

Hardcover: Scholastic
Published 1996

Two young boys, one white and one black, are taught the significance of the location where their new interracial community is being built. Their friendship would have been unimaginable in 1862, when the same ground was the site of a bitter Civil War battle. In this rhyming text, the two boys begin to appreciate the fact that they can now be friends and neighbors, and decide that their homes will stand as monuments to tolerance and freedom.

Patricia Mignon Hinds

AUTHOR

"When I was young, there were no books that reflected the breadth and beauty of our culture. We didn't have a selection of books showing children of color doing everyday things—living and learning. Being a curious child, I used to love to read Madeline stories. . . . I guess I identified with Madeline's independent spirit, especially her ability to take risks and to bounce back after getting herself into some pretty funny situations. I would have loved to have had storybooks about an African American little girl, like me, that I could read. But there weren't any."

OUR FAVORITE FROM
PATRICIA MIGNON HINDS

My Best Friend [61]

The Boy and the Ghost [105]

Written by Robert D. San Souci
Illustrated by J. Brian Pinkney

Hardcover: Simon & Schuster
Published 1989

> "*The ghost led the little boy to a lonely spot far from the house. Stopping under a huge sycamore tree, the ghost pointed with his right hand to the ground near its roots. 'Dig there,' he commanded.*"

Young Thomas leaves his parents' farm to find work to earn money for his struggling family. His parents offer him two simple pieces of advice as he departs: First, to always be polite and generous to everyone, and second, to always be brave and honest. When Thomas meets an old man along the way, he politely invites the other traveler to join him and then generously shares his small meal with the old fellow. The old man tells Thomas that he can earn a fortune if he is able to spend an entire night, from sunset to sunrise, in a haunted house on the hill. Thomas goes to the house and is confronted by the ghost, but remembers his parents' second lesson. Through his bravery and honesty, Thomas helps the ghost find eternal peace and wins the ghost's treasure.

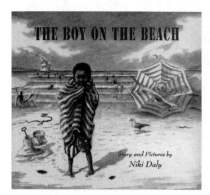

The Boy on the Beach [106]

Written and illustrated by Niki Daly

Hardcover: Margaret K. McElderry, Simon & Schuster
Published 1999

Young Joe accompanies his parents on a trip to the beach. The three enjoy an afternoon splashing and frolicking in the surf until Joe becomes bored and decides to run down the beach in search of something new. Before long he discovers an old abandoned boat, half buried in the sand, that becomes the stage for his imaginative adventure. But before he knows it, Joe looks up and realizes that he is lost among the sand dunes. His cries for help are answered by a new friend, who helps him reunite with his parents.

The Boy Who Didn't Believe in Spring [107]

Written by Lucille Clifton
Illustrated by Brinton Turkle

Softcover: Puffin, Penguin Putnam
Published 1973

King Shabazz is a very hip, street-wise kid. Based on his urban experience, he just doesn't believe in spring, the season of renewal. When he is told that spring is just around the corner, he decides to take a walk around the block with his best friend, just to see if he can find it. As the two walk the city streets, there is no trace of spring until they happen upon an empty lot, a very unlikely place to find spring. But evidence of the coming season abounds, changing the young boy's mind. **Nonstandard English.**

Brian's Bird [108]

Written by Patricia A. Davis
Illustrated by Layne Johnson

Hardcover: Albert Whitman
Published 2000

Eight-year-old Brian is surprised and delighted with his birthday present from his loving family—a parakeet. Brian, blind since early childhood, begins the intensive task of teaching his bird, Scratchy, to speak and to perch on his finger. Luckily Scratchy learns his lessons well. One day the bird flies outside through an open door, and Brian relies on his brother to guide him and on Scratchy to respond to his commands to recover his dear pet.

Brothers of the Knight [109]

Written by Debbie Allen
Illustrated by Kadir Nelson

Hardcover: Dial Books for Young Readers
Published 1999

Reverend Knight is unable to unravel a mystery in his own household. Every night his twelve sons go to bed behind a locked door and presumably sleep through the night. Yet every morning he finds twelve pairs of filthy, worn-out shoes at the foot of their beds. It takes a whimsical new nanny to solve the mystery. Young readers will enjoy this witty retelling of "The Twelve Dancing Princesses," narrated by the family dog, and the hip, colorful imagery of the illustrations.

> "*The brothers danced their way 'cross the rooftops. Steppin' and stompin'. The moon gave everything a magical glow, as if they were dancing on the Milky Way.*"

Buffalo Soldiers: The Story of Emanuel Stance [110]

Written by Robert Miller ☆104
Illustrated by Michael Bryant

Hardcover and softcover: Silver Press
Published 1995

This high-action story is about Emmanuel Stance, a member of the Ninth Calvary, one of the first all-black regiments in the United States Army. The Ninth Calvary, known as buffalo soldiers because their hair resembled that of the buffaloes, was chartered to protect pioneering settlers from the Indians. Stance distinguished himself as a leader and brave fighting soldier, and, in 1870, was the first black to receive the Congressional Medal of Honor. Two other books in this series about pioneering African Americans are *The Story of Jean Baptiste DuSable* [232] and *The Story of Nat Love*.

Calvin's Christmas Wish [111]

Written by Calvin Miles
Illustrated by Dolores Johnson

Hardcover and softcover: Penguin USA
Published 1993

Calvin is unnerved when his friend, W. C., tells him that Santa Claus does not really exist. Calvin has been counting on Santa Claus to bring him a new bicycle for Christmas, but now does not know what to expect. Calvin's Christmas wish does comes true, confirming that Santa exists after all! Remarkably, Calvin Miles wrote this book at the age of thirty-nine, shortly after learning to read and write with the help of the Literacy Volunteers of America.

Christopher, Please Clean Up Your Room! [112]

Written by Itah Sadu
Illustrated by Roy Condy

Softcover: Firefly
Published 1993

In this jovial story, young Christopher's room is such a mess that even the roaches won't go in. Despite pleas and warnings from his parents, Christopher steadfastly refuses to clean up his "funky" space. Finally, the goldfish, who live in a bowl of stagnant water in his room, make a pact with the roaches to convince Christopher to clean up his act. One night the roaches come by the thousands to Christopher's room. They cover him and his bed and then arrange themselves to spell out their instructions, "Christopher, tidy up your room now!" Terrified by the event, Christopher immediately jumps into action, cleaning, clearing, and picking up the mess.

Clean Your Room, Harvey Moon! [113]

Written and illustrated by Pat Cummings

Hardcover and softcover: Simon & Schuster
Published 1991

Harvey's messy room is deplorable, as described in this frolicking, rhyming verse. Harvey must clean up his hodgepodge before being allowed to watch any more television. This fun, colorfully illustrated poem will delight and entertain young readers.

Coming Home: From the Life of Langston Hughes [114]

Written and illustrated by Floyd Cooper

Hardcover: Philomel, Putnam
Published 1994

The early life story of renowned African American poet Langston Hughes is shared in this well-written biography. Langston's early disappointments, travails, and other experiences helped create the man whose poetic gifts grace African American literary history.

The Crab Man [115]

Written by Patricia E. Van West
Illustrated by Cedric Lucas ☆ 88

Hardcover: Turtle, Group West
Published 1998

Young Neville has a crisis of conscience when he discovers that the hermit crabs that he has been trapping for the crab man are being raced for the entertainment of tourists at a local resort. Dismayed by the cruelty, he steals back the crabs and chooses to let them go. His actions cost Neville his one dollar per day fee but buy him the knowledge that he did the right thing.

Angela
Johnson
AUTHOR

REFLECTIONS

"As a child I read a lot of comic books. I wasn't too interested in the books that were available to me in the library, although I did read anything that Ezra Jack Keats wrote. It wasn't until I was in middle school that I became a voracious book reader. Then I read more adult books and little young adult. I guess I truly never related to the children in the books the librarian was extolling. . . . As I now read incredible books with black and multicultural characters, I feel incredible."

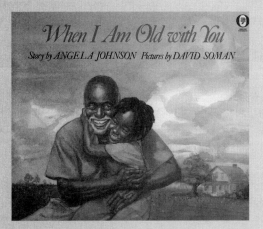

When I Am Old with You
Story by ANGELA JOHNSON Pictures by DAVID SOMAN

BLACK BOOKS GALORE!

OUR FAVORITES FROM
ANGELA JOHNSON

Daddy Calls Me Man [16]

Joshua by the Sea [51]

Joshua's Night Whispers [52]

Mama Bird, Baby Birds [54]

When I Am Old with You [82]

Creativity [116]

Written by John Steptoe
Illustrated by E. B. Lewis

Published by: Clarion, Houghton Mifflin
Published 1997

Charlie learns about the ancestry he has in common with the new boy at school. Hector's skin color and features are like Charlie's, but his hair is straight and he speaks Spanish. Charlie befriends Hector and tries to help him adjust to the new school and neighborhood. Charlie even intends to help Hector with his English, which amuses Charlie's father because Charlie uses a very creative form of the language himself! Fluid watercolor illustrations enrich the story of the new friendship. *Nonstandard English.*

The Day I Saw My Father Cry [117]

Written by Bill Cosby
Illustrated by Varnette P. Honeywood

Hardcover and softcover: Cartwheel, Scholastic
Published 2000

Young Bill and his family befriend a wonderful new neighbor, Alan Mills. Mr. Mills uses an inventive strategy to break up a fight between Bill and his brother, teaching the boys how to stop the conflict and work out cooperative solutions. Mr Mills's strategy works time and time again for young Bill and his friends. One day Bill comes home to find his father in tears. He has never before seen his father cry, and learns that Mr. Mills has died. Young readers learn a number of important life lessons in this sensitive short story. Other books in the Little Bill series include: *The Best Way to Play* [95], *The Day I Was Rich* [118], *The Meanest Thing to Say* [180], *Money Troubles* [184], *My Big Lie* [188], *One Dark and Scary Night* [206], *Shipwreck Sunday, Super-Fine Valentine* [237], *The Treasure Hunt* [241], and *The Worst Day of My Life* [257].

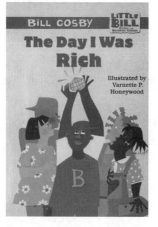

The Day I Was Rich [118]

Written by Bill Cosby
Illustrated by Varnette P. Honeywood

Hardcover and Softcover: Cartwheel, Scholastic
Published 1999

Little Bill is rich, if only for a day, when he discovers a huge glittering stone at the playground. He and his friends examine the huge gem and decide that it must be the largest diamond in the world, worth tens of millions of dollars. Since Little Bill has offered to share his wealth with his friends, they each imagine what they will do with their share. As it turns out, the discovery is only a glass paperweight, but the thrill of the possible was enough to make their day. Other books in the Little Bill series include *The Best Way to Play* [95], *The Day I Saw My Father Cry* [117], *The Meanest Thing to Say* [180], *Money Troubles* [184], *My Big Lie* [188], *One Dark and Scary Night* [206], *Shipwreck Sunday*, *Super-Fine Valentine* [237], *The Treasure Hunt* [241], and *The Worst Day of My Life* [257].

Dear Benjamin Banneker [119]

Written by Andrea Davis Pinkney
Illustrated by Brian Pinkney

Hardcover: Gulliver, Harcourt Brace
Published 1994

Benjamin Banneker, born free in 1731, was a brilliant, self-taught mathematician and astronomer who became known as America's first black man of science. Banneker was the first black man to write and publish an almanac, an almost impossible feat in his time. Additionally, he became one of the first civil rights activists, by corresponding with Thomas Jefferson, then the U.S. Secretary of State, to protest the enslavement of black people. This simple biography makes Banneker's story easily digestible for young readers.

Duke Ellington: The Piano Prince and His Orchestra [120]

Caldecott Honor Book
Coretta Scott King Honor: Illustrator

Written by Andrea Davis Pinkney
Illustrated by Brian Pinkney

Hardcover: Hyperion
Published 1998

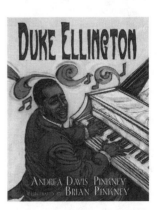

King of the Keys, Piano Prince, and Edward Kennedy Ellington are all names associated with the one and only Duke Ellington. This picture-book biography presents an overview of Ellington's magical career from his early days as a pianist in New York honky-tonks to his triumph as a composer and orchestra leader. Brightly colored scratchboard paintings help tell the story of the musical icon.

Elijah's Angel: A Story for Chanukah and Christmas [121]

Written by Michael J. Rosen
Illustrated by Aminah Brenda Lynn Robinson

Hardcover: Harcourt Brace Javonovich
Published 1992

Elijah, an eighty-year-old black barber, and Michael, a nine-year-old Jewish boy, are two unlikely friends in this unusual holiday story. Young Michael is intrigued by the beautiful wooden carvings that Elijah, an ex-slave, creates in his workshop. When Elijah offers the boy a wooden angel, Michael is disturbed because he believes the angel will be regarded as a "graven image" by his Jewish family. His parents help Michael understand that the angel need not have any religious significance and that he can accept it as simply a token of his friendship with the old man. This story is based on an event in the life of Elijah Pierce (1892–1984), an African American folk artist whose work is exhibited in the Columbus Museum of Art.

An Enchanted Hair Tale [122]

Written by Alexis DeVeaux
Illustrated by Cheryl Hanna

Coretta Scott King Honor: Author
Reading Rainbow **Review Book**

Softcover: HarperTrophy, HarperCollins
Published 1987

A young boy, Sudan, has a head full of "wild, mysterious" hair. His dreadlocks are so strange and so enchanted that children tease and grown-ups whisper, making Sudan ashamed of his misunderstood mane. Finally, Sudan meets a group of people with hair like his own. He learns to understand and enjoy what they have in common and to take pride in himself and his hair, setting an example of self-love for young readers. Fine black-and-white drawings illustrate the story.

Evan's Corner [123]

Written by Elizabeth Starr Hill
Illustrated by Sandra Speidel

Hardcover and softcover: Penguin USA
Published 1967

Evan, who lives with his large family in a small urban apartment, laments to his mother that he has no place to call his own. Mother allows Evan to claim one corner in the apartment for himself. He enthusiastically decorates his nook, establishing his new territory, but still finds that something is missing. Finally, he realizes that privacy is important but so is sharing and being with his family.

The Faithful Friend [124]

Written by Robert D. San Souci
Illustrated by Brian Pinkney

Caldecott Honor Book
Coretta Scott King Honor: Illustrator

Hardcover: Simon & Schuster
Published 1995

In this Caribbean folktale, Clement travels through Martinique accompanied by his best friend, Hippolyte, to seek the lovely Pauline's hand in marriage. Pauline's guardian, Monsieur Zabocat, reputed to be a wizard, is against the union and conjures up evil fates for the two. Hippolyte discovers the plots and sacrifices his own life to save his friends. Ultimately, good overcomes evil when Hippolyte's life is restored and the three friends are reunited.

> "*Hippolyte became a living person once more. . . . 'Your willingness to sacrifice your life for your friend gave me the power to break the spell, but a curse only ends when returned to its source.' *"

Fire on the Mountain [125]

Written by Jane Kurtz
Illustrated by E. B. Lewis

Hardcover: Simon & Schuster
Published 1994

A young Ethiopian boy accepts the challenge of his rich master to spend an entire night in the cold mountains with only a light cloak for warmth. If he succeeds, he will be rewarded. But if he fails, he and his sister will be banished. The boy successfully puts mind over matter, making it through the night by imagining that a fire, far off in the distance, is actually warming him. When he returns triumphantly, the master denounces the boy as a cheater for having taken comfort by the fire. In a humorous ending, the other servants, who resent the injustice, teach the master a practical lesson about fairness.

Fireflies for Nathan [126]

Written by Shulamith Levey Oppenheim
Illustrated by John Ward

Hardcover: Tambourine, William Morrow
Softcover: Puffin, Penguin USA
Published 1994

Six-year-old Nathan visits his grandparents in the country. They tell him boyhood stories about his father, who used to catch fireflies on summer evenings. Nathan convinces his grandparents to find the old firefly jar and to let him experience the magic. This is a pleasing story about the loving relationship between a child and his grandparents.

First Pink Light [127]

Written by Eloise Greenfield ☆ 42
Illustrated by Jan Spivey Gilchrist

Hardcover and softcover: Black Butterfly, Writers & Readers
Published 1976

Tyree misses his daddy, who has been away on business for a month. Tyree insists on waiting up for Daddy's arrival, not expected until dawn, just after the first pink light. Wisely, his mother gives up the bedtime battle, but she wins the war by convincing Tyree to put on his pajamas and to curl up on the couch to wait. Tyree falls asleep, as expected, missing the first pink light and Daddy's actual arrival but none of the joy of the reunion. Mother's wisdom and family love are prominent themes in this story.

For the Love of the Game: Michael Jordan and Me [128]

Written by Eloise Greenfield ☆ 42
Illustrated by Jan Spivey Gilchrist

Hardcover: HarperCollins
Published 1997

Michael Jordan loves to play basketball and uses his God-given talent to excel at his game. In an analogy between themselves and Michael Jordan, two children realize that they can use their own special talents to achieve great things in their own lives. The children recognize that life may hold obstacles and challenges, but they understand that they can rise above them and soar toward their own goals, the way Michael Jordan soars to the basket. Young Jordan fans will enjoy the basketball scenes.

The Fortune-Tellers [129]

Written by Lloyd Alexander
Illustrated by Trina Schart Hyman

Hardcover and softcover: Penguin USA
Published 1992

A restless young carpenter seeks counsel from a fraudulent fortune-teller. The fortune-teller answers in ambiguous double-talk, leading the young man to believe in the incredible predictions about his future. In a turn of events, the fortune-teller's luck changes for the worse, while the young carpenter becomes a fortune-teller himself and manages to realize all of the fortunes that were foretold. Both story and illustrations are witty and entertaining.

The Freedom Riddle [130]

Adapted by Angela Shelf Medearis
Illustrated by John Ward

Hardcover: Lodestar, Penguin USA
Published 1995

It was a Christmas tradition on Master Brown's plantation that the first person to say "Christmas gift" to another on Christmas day would receive a gift. Jim, a slave, approaches his master and is first with the phrase, thus entitling himself to a present. Rather than the usual gift, Jim asks for his own freedom if he is able to pose an unsolvable riddle. Master Brown agrees to the challenge. It takes Jim over a year to decide upon the riddle, but he finally presents one that stumps his master and earns him liberation.

Jabrille Williams, age 7

"I like *A Is for Africa* because it tells you a lot about Africa, and I also like the Little Bill books."

THE CREATOR'S

Dolores Johnson
AUTHOR AND ILLUSTRATOR

"I loved to read as a child, but did not have a lot of children's books around me. The only books that I owned as a child that stand out in my memory are Golden Books and books about a girl heroine named Cherry Ames. While I really enjoyed those books, I mostly just enjoyed reading. . . . I am particularly grateful that there is so much literature available for children of all colors today. I can only imagine how wide my world would have expanded if I had been able to read about and see pictures in books about a little girl like me."

OUR FAVORITES FROM
DOLORES JOHNSON

Grandma's Hands [135]

My Mom Is My Show-and-Tell [193]

What Kind of Baby-Sitter Is This? [249]

Your Dad Was Just Like You [258]

Galimoto [131]

Written by Karen Lynn Williams
Illustrated by Catherine Stock

Reading Rainbow Feature Book

Hardcover and softcover: William Morrow
Published 1990

Kondi, a young African boy, spends a day gathering scrap wire so that he can make a *galimoto,* a push toy made from sticks and wires. Kondi must scavenge for the materials in order to complete his new toy. This story demonstrates the rewards of tenacity and sticking to your goals.

Gettin' Through Thursday [132]

Written by Melrose Cooper
Illustrated by Nneka Bennett

Hardcover: Lee & Low
Published 1998

Money is always tight by the time Thursday comes along, because Mama doesn't get paid until Friday. Every Thursday is the same—the family always runs out of something and Mama has to help them find a way to make do, like the time she taught them to use baking soda when the toothpaste ran out. When André brings home an honor roll report card on a Thursday, he is disappointed because he knows that there will be no money to sponsor the celebration of his accomplishment. But Mama comes through with her most creative and loving improvisation to save the day.

Gift of the Sun: A Tale from South Africa [133]

Written by Dianne Stewart
Illustrated by Jude Daly

Hardcover: Farrar, Straus and Giroux
Published 1996

Thulani, a rural South African farmer, is bored by milking his cow, so he trades it for a goat. The goat eats up all of Thulani's seeds, so he trades it for a sheep. Shearing the sheep is too much work, so Thulani continues to make trades until he is left with only a bag of sunflower seeds. Inadvertently, the sunflowers seeds bring a new form of prosperity to the farmer and his wife in this frolicsome story.

Granddaddy's Street Songs [134]

Written by Monalisa DeGross
Illustrated by Floyd Cooper

Hardcover: Jump at the Sun, Hyperion
Published 1999

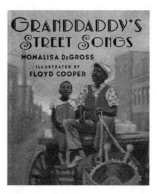

Roddy joins his grandfather, a street produce vendor (an "arabber"), for a day on the streets of Baltimore. As they travel their route, calling out their lyrical songs to attract customers, "Wa-a-a-ter-melons, I got wa-a-a-termelons. Come git my wa-a-ter-melons," Roddy enjoys looking at an old photo album and hearing stories from Granddaddy about the good old days. The affection between the two is apparent in the soft watercolor illustrations. ***Nonstandard English.***

Grandma's Hands [135]

Written and illustrated by Dolores Johnson ☆ 72

Hardcover: Marshall Cavendish
Published 1998

A young boy is delivered to his Grandma's farm by his mother when she decides that she must leave him for a while to "get herself together." At first the transition is difficult. He misses his mother, and Grandma is coarse and doesn't smile very often. But over time the grandmother and child bond through shared meals, chores, and meaningful talks. When his mother comes to get him many months later, he feels that he is being torn away again, from a home he has come to love and from Grandma's rough but loving hands.

Grandpa, Is Everything Black Bad? [136]

Written by Sandy Lynne Holman
Illustrated by Lela Kometiani

Hardcover: Culture Co-Op
Published 1998

Young Montsho becomes insecure about his own blackness when he observes that the color black seems to represent the worst—black and scary, black for funerals, black cats, and black sheep. He asks his grandpa, "Is everything black bad?" Grandpa wisely affirms Montsho by telling him about their proud black heritage, rooted in Africa, including stories about the dark-skinned Africans who developed writing, mathematics, calendars, astronomy, and religion and who built the great pyramids.

"Be proud of your dark skin. It represents a proud people and black is truly a beautiful color. It was passed down to you by Africans who lived before and your heritage is like no other."

Grandpa's Visit [137]

Written by Richardo Keens-Douglas
Illustrated by Frances Clancy

Hardcover and softcover: Annick
Published 1996

High-tech Jeremy, who is hooked on computers, VCRs, and video games, and his career-oriented parents are a typical modern family. Grandpa makes a surprise visit and is alarmed by the impersonal family dynamics. When the electricity goes off one evening, Grandpa uses the occasion to engage the family in a playful evening with a rubber ball. The family reconnects and is reminded of the simple pleasure of sharing one another's company. This is a timely story that may remind both young readers and their families about their real priority: each other!

Gregory Cool [138]

Written and illustrated by Caroline Binch

Hardcover: Dial, Penguin USA
Published 1994

An all-American preadolescent, Gregory experiences culture shock when he visits his grandparents in Tobago for a four-week vacation. The weather, food, and daily life are just too different and too uncool for Gregory. As his vacation goes on he is suddenly struck by how much fun one can have doing "uncool" things. Gregory is just a kid at heart, who, like your own youngster, can afford a little more time in his childhood.

Haircuts at Sleepy Sam's [139]

Written by Michael R. Strickland
Illustrated by Keaf Holliday

Hardcover: Boyds Mills
Published 1998

Three attractively illustrated brothers get a delightful surprise when they take their weekly trip to Sleepy Sam's Barber Shop. Every week their mom gives them each a note, directing Sam to give them an Afro-cut. But Afro-cuts are old fashioned, and the boys want a fresher look. Today is their day, when Sleepy Sam takes the initiative to update their look to the more popular bald fade.

Happy Birthday, Dr. King! [140]

Written by Kathryn Jones
Illustrated by Floyd Cooper

Softcover: Simon & Schuster
Published 1994

After getting in trouble at school for fighting with another boy because he wanted to sit in the back seat of the bus, fourth-grader Jamal gets in trouble again at home when his Grandpa Joe learns about the scuffle. Grandpa Joe explains the story of Rosa Parks and the Montgomery bus boycott to help Jamal understand the history associated with sitting in the back of the bus. Jamal is so impressed with the story that he leads his class in a skit about the historic incident, which they stage in celebration of Martin Luther King Jr.'s birthday.

Happy Birthday, Martin Luther King [141]

Written by Jean Marzollo
Illustrated by Brian J. Pinkney

Hardcover and softcover: Scholastic
Published 1993

The life story of Martin Luther King Jr. is told in this elementary reader. The details of King's birth, education, life's work, and legacy are introduced to young children in storybook style to help them understand the importance of this monumental figure.

Hard to Be Six [142]

Written by Arnold Adoff
Illustrated by Cheryl Hanna

Hardcover: Lothrop, Lee & Shepard, William Morrow
Published 1990

A young boy is frustrated because being six years old does not live up to his expectations. There are still too many things that he cannot do that his ten-year-old sister can. His sensitive grandmother tunes in to his problem and successfully helps him understand how important it is to accept and enjoy the privileges, responsibilities, and opportunities of each age. You may enjoy sharing this story with your own children who are often too anxious to grow up!

The Hatseller and the Monkeys [143]

Written and illustrated by Baba Wagué Diakité

Hardcover: Scholastic
Published 1999

BaMusa, a West African hatseller, uses a little monkey psychology when a group of the mischievous creatures threatens his business. While he rests under a mango tree, a family of monkeys descends upon the sleeping merchant and steals all of the hats he intends to sell at the market. When he discovers his loss, he yells up at the monkeys, but they just yell back. He throws a branch and then stones at them, but they just throw mangoes back. Cleverly BaMusa decides upon a plan of action to retrieve his merchandise. Young readers will laugh at BaMusa's dilemma, which can easily be play-acted for more fun. Colorful Afrocentric illustrations accompany this delightful tale.

The Hired Hand: An African American Folktale [144]

Retold by Robert D. San Souci
Illustrated by Jerry Pinkney

Hardcover: Dial
Published 1997

Young Sam is shiftless, lazy, and no help to his father, Old Sam, at their saw mill. He is so worthless that Old Sam hires a man to pick up the slack. Young Sam treats the new hired hand badly, ordering him around and criticizing his work. But one day young Sam witnesses the hired hand performing a miraculous deed, magically returning an old man to his youth. Young Sam tries to use the secret incantation for his own profit, but the results are disastrous. This original African American folktale offers a dramatic lesson of virtue for young readers. **Nonstandard English.**

> **"**Young Sam wouldn't lift a finger. He put all the work on the hired man, then called him lazy and yelled at him to work faster.**"**

Hoops [145]

Written by Robert Burleigh
Illustrated by Stephen T. Johnson

Hardcover: Silver Whistle, Harcourt Brace
Published 1997

Even if you have never played basketball, you will know exactly how it feels
to hold the ball and run the court after reading this articulate poem about
the game. Young readers will feel the tension, the excitement, and the physical actions of a player through the crisp text and the action-filled illustrations of the game in play.

The House in the Sky: A Bahamian Folktale [146]

Written by Robert D. San Souci
Illustrated by Wil Clay

Hardcover: Dial, Penguin USA
Published 1996

This traditional Caribbean folktale tells the story of two lazy brothers who
discover a magical abode in the sky that belongs to the spirit folk. While the
spirit folk are away during the day, the brothers sneak into the house and steal
all the food their hearts desire. One brother, though lazy, is still clever enough
to eat and run. The other is both lazy and greedy, so he gets caught. Young
readers will enjoy the drama and suspense and be thrilled by the unusual
appearance of the spirit folk. *Caribbean dialect.*

How Many Stars in the Sky? [147]

Written by Lenny Hort   **Reading Rainbow Review Book**
Illustrated by James E. Ransome

Hardcover: Tambourine
Published 1991

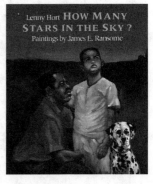

A curious young boy tries to count the stars in the sky from his suburban
home, but the task is too overwhelming. So Daddy takes him for a long ride,
through the glare of the city lights, into the country where the view is better.
The two share a special night during their impossible task, but the experience bonds them in countless other ways in this richly illustrated, warm story.

Julius
Lester

AUTHOR

"I had no favorite books as a child. I read eclectically, primarily books on geography, history, and biographies, as well as tons of comic books.

"There is so much available today . . . but because I enjoy history and biographies, I read the work of Jim Haskins and the McKissacks. Their books would certainly have been welcome when I was a boy."

OUR FAVORITES FROM
JULIUS LESTER

*Black Cowboy, Wild Horses:
A True Story* [102]

John Henry [156]

*Sam and the Tigers: A New Retelling
of Little Black Sambo* [220]

Hue Boy [148]

Written by Rita Phillips Mitchell
Illustrated by Caroline Binch

Hardcover and softcover: Penguin USA
Published 1993

"*And Hue boy walked tall, with his head held high. He was the happiest boy in the village. And he didn't feel small at all, at all.*"

Hue is the smallest boy on his Caribbean island. His mother is concerned about his lack of growth, so she takes him to see the island's wise man, the doctor, and even Miss Frangipnia, who casts a spell over his head and gives him bathing herbs to make him grow. Still, Hue Boy does not grow. When he sees his Papa disembarking from a ship after several long months away at sea, he walks taller than he ever has with the pride of a loving son.

I Can Do It by Myself [149]

Written by Lessie Jones Little and Eloise Greenfield ☆ 42
Illustrated by Carole Byard

Hardcover: Thomas Y. Crowell
Published 1978

Donny is going shopping today for his mother's birthday gift. On his way out he was offended by his older brother's offer to go with him, as if he wasn't old enough to go shopping alone. Then his mother seemed anxious when he announced he was going out. Then two old ladies on the street called him cute, as if he was a baby. Finally, the clerk at the stored demeaned him by calling him "kid." Donny would have taken it all again, if any one of them had been there when, on the way back from the store, he was confronted by a bulldog. But instead he had to stand up and deal with this threatening situation like a big boy!

I Have a Dream: Dr. Martin Luther King, Jr. [150]

Written by Martin Luther King Jr.
Illustrated by various artists

Hardcover: Scholastic
Published 1997

Martin Luther King Jr.'s moving "I Have A Dream" speech is revisited in this beautiful commemorative book. Exquisite illustrations by fifteen talented winners of the Coretta Scott King Award—including Ashley Bryan, Tom Feelings, Pat Cummings, and James Ransome—bring Dr. King's speech to life for young readers, who may be reading these thirty-year-old words for the first time. Coretta Scott King has written a beautifully simple foreword introducing her husband's 1963 speech, and at the back of the book, each illustrator describes his artistic depiction of scenes from the Martin Luther King Jr. era.

> **"I** *have a dream that my four little children will one day live in a nation where they will not be judged by the color of their skin but by the content of their character. I have a dream today!"*

If I Only Had a Horn: Young Louis Armstrong [151]

Written by Roxane Orgill
Illustrated by Leonard Jenkins

Hardcover: Houghton Mifflin
Published 1997

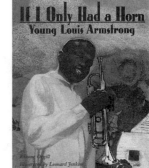

Some kids know from a very early age what they want to be. Louis Armstrong was one of those, and this story tells about his journey from juvenile delinquent to legendary musician. Louis's interest was born from the streets of New Orleans, where he grew up, and then brought to fruition in a detention center for boys, where he was a member of the band. The illustrations in this book are superbly presented with sharp imagery on muted backgrounds.

Imani and the Flying Africans [152]

Written by Janice Liddell
Illustrated by Linda Nickens

Hardcover: Africa World
Published 1994

While on a road trip from Detroit to Savannah to visit his grandparents and great-grandmother, Imani's mama tells him the incredible story of the Flying Africans. The story, which is still a well-known myth among the African Americans of Georgia's Sea Islands, is about the rebellious African slaves who escaped slavery by actually flying away to Africa. During the telling of the story, Imani learns for the first time that his great-grandmother was once a slave, a revelation that leads him to a surreal dream adventure and encounter with the wise old woman.

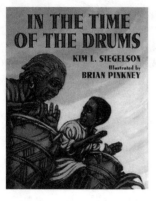

In the Time of the Drums [153]

Written by Kim L. Siegelson   Coretta Scott King Award: Illustrator
Illustrated by Brian Pinkney

Hardcover: Jump at the Sun, Hyperion
Published 1999

In this story, passed down through the oral tradition of the Sea Island Gullahs, an African-born slave woman, Twi, takes a young boy, Mentu, under her wing. Twi loves and mentors Mentu as if he were her very own. She teaches him about his African heritage, including the music of the drums, and implores him to grow into a strong man who will never let go of his culture. When a slave ship full of Ibo tribesmen lands, Twi joins the rebellious Ibos, leading them into the water for their long walk, across the ocean floor, back to their homeland. Mentu is left behind to testify to the events and to keep the African traditions alive for his people.

Jackson Jones and the Puddle of Thorns [154]

Written by Mary Quattlebaum
Illustrated by Melodye Rosales

Hardcover: Delacorte, Bantam Doubleday Dell
Published 1994

Instead of the basketball he expected, Jackson Jones is given a garden patch for his tenth birthday. What was a ten-year-old boy supposed to do with a garden patch? Jackson's entrepreneurial spirit, however, is quickly aroused as he realizes that he can grow flowers and sell them, thereby earning enough money to buy himself the basketball. But there are problems along the way— jealous friends, a taunting bully, and gardening problems. Young readers will enjoy Jackson's challenges and how he rises to the occasion in this witty story.

Jimmy Lee Did It [155]

Written and illustrated by Pat Cummings

Hardcover: Lothrop, Lee & Shepard, William Morrow
Softcover: HarperTrophy, HarperCollins
Published 1985

This colorful primary reader follows the mysterious mischief of Jimmy Lee. Nobody is quite sure who Jimmy Lee is or what he looks like, but evidence of his misdeeds abounds. There are spills and tears, drawings on the wall, and other troublesome things that seem to happen only when Artie is around. Artie blames everything on the phantom, Jimmy Lee. Young readers will enjoy speculating about the culprit and solving the mystery of Jimmy Lee.

John Henry [156]

Written by Julius Lester ☆ 80
Illustrated by Jerry Pinkney

Caldecott Honor Book

Hardcover: Dial, Penguin USA
Published 1994

Nobody knows for sure whether John Henry was a real or a fictitious character, but it is said that he was the biggest and strongest man ever. According to the legend, John Henry competed successfully against a steam drill while breaking ground for the railroad in West Virginia. The intense illustrations of the laboring Henry convey the strength of his character. The story is written perfectly for an animated read-aloud about this larger-than-life character.

> **"H**e had a twenty-pound hammer in each hand and
> muscles hard as wisdom in each arm. As he swung
> them through the air, they shone like silver, and when
> the hammers hit the rock, they rang like gold."

Joshua's Masai Mask [157]

Written by Dakari Hru
Illustrated by Anna Rich

Hardcover and softcover: Lee & Low
Published 1993

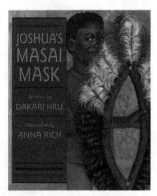

Joshua is insecure about competing in the school talent show, where he plans to play the kalimba, an African instrument. He fears his performance will not be as spectacular as the dancing and rapping of some of his classmates. Joshua's uncle gives him a Masai mask to help him get into the spirit of the performance, but warns that the mask has magical powers. The mask magically transplants Joshua into the bodies of the classmates whom he envies. His brief experiences in other people's shoes prove to him, and will show young readers, that it is best to be oneself.

Journey to Freedom: A Story of the Underground Railroad [158]

Written by Cournti C. Wright
Illustrated by Gershom Griffith

Hardcover: Holiday
Published 1994

"*W*hen the first
joy and excite-
ment of freedom are
over, Miss Tubman
leads us in a prayer
of thanksgiving to
God.*"*

Barefoot and threadbare, young Joshua and Nathan and their parents travel the Underground Railroad with Harriet Tubman as their conductor. For twenty treacherous days and nights the group treks from their Kentucky plantation to freedom in Canada, eluding slave catchers, coping with hunger and fear, and braving the season's first snow. The family's passion for each other and for their freedom motivates them to push ahead with the challenging journey.

Julian, Secret Agent [159]

Written by Ann Cameron
Illustrated by Diane Allison

Softcover: Stepping Stone, Random House
Published 1988

Julian, his brother Huey, and his friend Gloria become would-be crime busters when they try to catch a bank robber with a $25,000 reward on his head. As the three track their man, they are in and out of trouble in a series of entertaining adventures, including saving a drowning child and rescuing a dog stuck in a hot car. Julian's adventures are told in four other books: *Julian, Dream Doctor; Julian's Glorious Summer* [160]*; More Stories Julian Tells;* and *The Stories Julian Tells.*

Julian's Glorious Summer [160]

Written by Ann Cameron
Illustrated by Dora Leder

Softcover: Stepping Stone, Random House
Published 1987

Poor Julian! His best friend, Gloria, has a new bike and is riding all over the neighborhood, and Julian has not even learned to ride a bike yet.

Embarrassed by his shortcoming, Julian does everything he can to avoid Gloria and then, to cover himself, tells a little fib that grows to incredible heights in this delightful, easy-to-read story. There are several books in the series about young Julian, including *Julian, Dream Doctor; Julian, Secret Agent* [159]; *More Stories Julian Tells;* and *The Stories Julian Tells.*

Juma and the Honey Guide: An African Story [161]

Written by Robin Bernard
Illustrated by Nneka Bennett

Hardcover: Silver Press
Published 1996

Bakari and Juma, father and son, travel through the African bush to find honey. They carefully track and follow the honey-guide bird, which will lead them to their sweet reward. The bird leads them to an acacia tree bearing a huge beehive. The two patiently smoke out the bees and remove the hive full of honey. As they prepare to go home, Bakari admonishes Juma to put a piece of the honeycomb back in the tree for the bird as a reward for helping them find the hive. Juma selfishly refuses until his father gives him a profound reason to obey, and young readers a reason to snicker.

Keepers [162]

Written by Jeri Hanel Watts
Illustrated by Felicia Marshall

Hardcover: Lee & Low
Published 1997

Young Kenyon lives with his father and Little Dolly, his almost ninety-year-old grandma, who often entertains Kenyon with stories that she has carried down from the past generations. As a keeper of stories, she is looking for someone she can trust from the succeeding generation to be the next keeper. Kenyon would love the job, but he betrays a trust when he misappropriates the money that was set aside for Little Dolly's birthday party. Determined to make amends, Kenyon creates a handmade book of Little Dolly's stories, demonstrating that he can be a trusted keeper.

Cedric
Lucas
ILLUSTRATOR

"Some of my favorite books as a child came from Dr. Seuss and Ezra Jack Keats. Some of my favorite books were *Whistle for Willie, Snowy Day,* and the Cat in the Hat series. I would have liked to see more black characters and that's why I enjoyed Keats's books."

OUR FAVORITES FROM
CEDRIC LUCAS

The Crab Man [115]

Frederick Douglass: The Last Days of Slavery [288]

Night Golf [201]

Kele's Secret [163]

Written by Tololwa M. Mollel
Illustrated by Catherine Stock

Hardcover: Lodestar
Published 1997

Yoanes, a young Tanzanian boy, is motivated by the treat he will earn if he helps his grandmother find the eggs that her chicken, Kele, is laying. The secretive chicken has been laying her eggs all over the farm—in the loft, the barn, and even the outhouse. Grandmother is anxious to find all of the eggs so she can take them to market to sell. Yoanes follows the fowl all day, watching her every move, until he discovers her secret place, a scary shed overgrown with vines. Yoanes must overcome his fears, which are fed by an overactive imagination, to enter the dark place to find Kele's nest.

Kevin and His Dad [164]

Written by Irene Smalls ☆ 160
Illustrated by Michael Hays

Hardcover: Little, Brown
Published 1999

Kevin spends a special day with his dad while his mom is away. The two spend a day full of shared activities like vacuuming, cleaning windows, and laundering. But there is still time after their chores to play. The two play ball and even take in a movie. This story, told in rhyme, sets an excellent example of male responsibility and male bonding.

Kobe Bryant [165]

Written by Richard J. Brenner

Softcover: Beech Tree, William Morrow
Published 1999

Very young basketball fans will quickly devour this book about Kobe Bryant, the popular and exciting NBA All-Star player who plays for the Los Angeles Lakers. Large print and a large selection of game-action photographs, including a slam-dunking centerfold of Kobe, tell about his professional career in the game he loves. *Michael Jordan,* a second book in this easy-to-read series, is also available.

Kofi and His Magic [166]

Written by Maya Angelou
Photographed by Margaret Courtney-Clarke

Hardcover: Clarkson Potter, Crown
Published 1996

A seven-year-old boy named Kofi tells the story of his West African village of Bonwire, which is known for the beautiful kente cloth that is woven there. Kofi magically transports young readers to other sites in his country, showing them the best and most beautiful parts of his land. Colorful photographs of the people and sights of Bonwire illustrate the story. Young readers who know about kente cloth will now understand more about its origin and the magic of its creation. A companion title, *My Painted House, My Friendly Chicken, and Me,* is another wonderful photographic essay about village life in Africa.

Koi and the Kola Nuts: A Tale from Liberia [167]

Written by Verna Aardema
Illustrated by Joe Cepeda

Hardcover: Atheneum Books for Young Readers
Published 1999

Young Koi, the son of a chief, strikes out to explore the world with his only inheritance, a bag of kola nuts. He encounters a snake, an army of ants, and a crocodile, all in need of his nuts to solve their own problems. Koi gives the nuts freely, even though they are all he has. Later Koi enters a village and accepts the village chief's challenge to perform three impossible tasks. If he is successful, he will win the hand of the chief's daughter; if not, he will die. Koi's earlier kindness is rewarded when the creatures he once helped return to help him, proving the adage, "Do good and good will come back to you—in full measure and overflowing."

Lake of the Big Snake: An African Rain Forest Adventure [168]

Written by Isaac Olaleye
Illustrated by Claudia Shepard

Hardcover: Boyds Mills
Published 1998

Two young Nigerian boys, Ada and Tayo, are the best of friends. In this engaging, fast-paced story, the two are threatened by a large water snake as they frolic in the river. Their mothers had warned them not to leave the village, and their disobedience has led them into this dangerous situation. The two friends try to hide and to outsmart the snake. But it takes all of their wits to come up with a plan that saves them both. It seems that nothing, however, will save them from their scolding mothers when they return to the village.

Leagues Apart: The Men and Times of the Negro Baseball Leagues [169]

Written by Lawrence S. Ritter
Illustrated by Richard Merkin

Softcover: Mulberry, William Morrow
Published 1995

The stories of twenty of baseball's African American trailblazers, most of whom never had the chance to play in the major leagues because they were black, are briefly outlined in this book for young sports fans. Each of the historical characters, who played for the love of the game, is illustrated with a simple description of his game attributes.

Let Freedom Ring: A Ballad of Martin Luther King, Jr. [170]

Written by Myra Cohn Livingston
Illustrated by Samuel Byrd

Hardcover: Holiday
Published 1992

Profound quotes from some of the many famous speeches made by Martin Luther King Jr. are poetically woven together into a ballad telling the story of the civil rights leader's life. The refrain, "From every mountain, let freedom ring," captures the essence of King's life work. Provocative illustrations of King with both his supporters and his antagonists are deeply reminiscent of his time.

Little Cliff and the Porch People [171]

Written by Clifton L. Taulbert
Illustrated by E. B. Lewis

Hardcover: Dial
Published 1999

Little Cliff was supposed to go straight up the road to Miz Callie's house to buy a pound of special butter for Mama Pearl. Mama Pearl was going to turn ordinary sweet potatoes into her famous candy potatoes with the right ingredients and a little of her magic. Along the way, each of Cliff's neighbors stops the young boy for a chat and to offer him another ingredient for Mama Pearl to add to the potatoes—vanilla, nutmeg, and fresh fat. Cliff finally completes his mission, and Mama Pearl keeps her promise to make him the sweetest, softest candied potatoes ever. Then Cliff happily shares them with his good neighbors. **Nonstandard English.**

Jordan T. Perry, age 7

"I really liked *The Fortune-Tellers* when I was little and now I like books by Faith Ringgold."

Little Eight John [172]

Written by Jan Wahl
Illustrated by Wil Clay

Coretta Scott King Honor: Illustrator

Hardcover: Lodestar, Dutton
Published 1992

Little Eight John is full of mischief, disobeying every caution that his mother and father give him. Superstitiously, they warn him that bad luck will befall the family if he sits backward on the chair, counts his teeth, or sleeps with his head at the foot of the bed. But the rebellious youth does all these things and more, to the regret of his family, who suffer the aftermath of each action. It is only when Little Eight John faces his own hard consequences that he accepts his parents' wisdom and agrees to change his ways.

Little Muddy Waters: A Gullah Folk Tale [173]

Written by Ronald Daise
Illustrated by Barbara McArtor

Hardcover: G.O.G. Enterprises
Published 1997

Little Muddy Waters, so named in the Gullah tradition because of his good looks and dark skin, is a "don't-listen-to-anybody, do-whatever-he-wanted-to-do little child." His frustrated grandparents often chide Little Muddy Waters to "respect yo elders and do what's right." But he goes out of his way to disobey the good advice. Sometimes his mischief is downright mean, as when he purposely violates a household superstition and brings bad luck upon his entire family. The boy finally learns his lesson, the hard way, when he is rude to an old man. Young readers will enjoy the story told in colorful Gullah dialect about this mischievous young boy and the day he meets his match. **Nonstandard English.**

The Longest Wait [174]

Written by Marie Bradby
Illustrated by Peter Catalanotto

Hardcover: Orchard
Published 1998

Young Thomas is left at home to worry about his father, a mail carrier who is out in a blizzard delivering the mail. Daddy is gone for a long time in the treacherous storm, while Thomas and the rest of the family worry about him. Eventually Daddy does return, but he becomes deliriously ill from exposure to the weather. All night Thomas worries, hoping that Daddy will recover. In the morning Thomas knows that it will be all right. Daddy awakens and the two are able to go out to sled in the brilliant newly fallen snow. *Nonstandard English.*

Ma Dear's Aprons [175]

Written by Patricia C. McKissack ☆ 96
Illustrated by Floyd Cooper

Hardcover: Atheneum, Simon & Schuster
Published 1997

This lovely story pays tribute to the black women of earlier generations who worked tirelessly as domestic workers but still had time to love and care for their own families. In this sweet story, David Earl learns to tell the day of the week by the color and style of his mother's apron. She has one for every day of the week, except Sunday, her day off—the day she spends with him.

The Magic Tree: A Folktale from Nigeria [176]

Written by T. Obinkaram Echewa
Illustrated by E. B. Lewis

Hardcover: William Morrow
Published 1999

Mbi, an orphan boy, lives with his unkind relatives in an African village. He is overworked, underloved, and underfed by his family and the other villagers, and called upon only when there is work to do. As Mbi sits under an udara tree, it magically begins to bear delicious, but unseasonable, fruit for him to eat. When he plants the seeds from the fruit, another full-grown, fruit-laden tree grows within minutes. Mbi discovers that he is able to direct the tree to grow, bear more fruit, or raise and lower its branches with a magical song. He also discovers that he can command a new respect from the villagers with his new-found powers.

Patricia
McKissack

AUTHOR

"My favorite books were fantasy—fairy tales, myths, and legends—stories from all over the world, about people who lived in another time and place, far away from the day-to-day prejudices and racism of the 1950s. Anthropomorphic stories were also fun to read because no race was involved, only animals who talked and acted like people—and sometimes like family and friends. I think Hans Christian Andersen's 'The Ugly Duckling' has always been special. I never really knew why. But recently I came to realize I must have recognized the metaphor instinctively—that like the little duckling, we as a race would one day come into our own and be recognized for the beautiful people we are.

"Oh, if I had had the illustrations of Jerry and Brian Pinkney, Floyd Cooper, James Ransome, Pat Cummings, and Wil Clay, I probably would have read more. . . . If Virginia Hamilton, Mildred Taylor, Joyce Hansen and others had been writing in the 1950s, I might have learned a lot earlier to read for enjoyment. In their books, little brothers and sisters learn that a smart black person who knows his or her history is worthy of admiration—the stuff that makes good heroes."

OUR FAVORITES FROM
PATRICIA McKISSACK

Black Diamond: The Story of the Negro Baseball Leagues [269]

Black Hands, White Sails: The Story of African-American Whalers [270]

Ma Dear's Aprons [175]

A Million Fish . . . More or Less [182]

Malcolm X [177]

Written by Arnold Adoff
Illustrated by John Wilson

Hardcover: HarperTrophy, HarperCollins
Published 1970

The life and times of Malcolm X are explored in elementary terms for young readers. The brief biography touches on Malcolm's life from his birth to Reverend and Mrs. Earl Little in 1925 through his assassination in 1965. Young readers will understand the political and spiritual journey that motivated Malcolm and distinguished him as an African American icon.

Mandela: From the Life of the South African Statesman [178]

Written and illustrated by Floyd Cooper

Hardcover: Philomel, Putnam
Published 1996

In this simple but accurate account of the life of Nelson Mandela, a young reader will learn about Mandela's education and personal development from early childhood until the time that he became the president of South Africa. This book is a valuable guide to understanding who Mandela is and how he became such a great leader.

Max Found Two Sticks [179]

Written and illustrated by Brian Pinkney   ***Reading Rainbow** Review Book*

Hardcover and softcover: Simon & Schuster
Published 1994

Max finds two heavy sticks on the ground, which he employs to tap out rhythmic answers to questions in lieu of speaking. He "rah-tah-tah-tahs" and "thmps-di-di-thmps" all day long, communicating and imitating the beats of the city's sounds. The foot-tapping text matches the upbeat illustrations.

The Meanest Thing to Say [180]

Written by Bill Cosby
Illustrated by Varnette P. Honeywood

Hardcover and softcover: Cartwheel, Scholastic
Published 1997

Little Bill learns a valuable lesson in interpersonal skills and self-control when he refuses to be drawn into a game of "playing the dozens" with a new boy at school. The new boy, Michael, tries to taunt Little Bill into an angry reaction, but Little Bill exercises a simple nonconfrontational strategy that sees him through the experience. Later, Little Bill shows more strength of character when he invites Michael to play, even after the embarrassing showdown. Other books in the Little Bill series include *The Best Way to Play* [95], *The Day I Saw My Father Cry* [117], *The Day I Was Rich* [118], *Money Troubles* [184], *My Big Lie* [188], *One Dark and Scary Night* [206], *Shipwreck Sunday*, *Super-Fine Valentine* [237], *The Treasure Hunt* [241], and *The Worst Day of My Life* [257].

Meet Martin Luther King, Jr.: A Man of Peace with a Dream for All People [181]

Written by James T. deKay

Softcover: Bullseye, Random House
Published 1993

The story of Dr. Martin Luther King Jr. is revealed to young readers in this elementary-level chapter book. Dr. King's life is told from his childhood, when racist experiences had already begun to shape his thinking, through his assassination in 1968. Virtually every major milestone in Dr. King's life and career is simply shared in this comprehensive book, which answers most of the questions regarding his life's work as a civil rights leader.

A Million Fish . . . More or Less [182]

Written by Patricia C. McKissack ☆ 96
Illustrated by Dena Schultzer

Hardcover: Alfred A. Knopf
Softcover: Dragonfly, Alfred A. Knopf
Published 1992

Young Hugh didn't know whether to believe Papa-Daddy and Elder Abbajon or not when they told him that they caught a five-hundred-pound turkey, more or less, and other incredible tales about their adventures in the Bayou Clapateaux. And the two old men didn't know whether to believe Hugh when he returned home after a fishing trip in the bayou with only three fish but an equally incredible story about the one million fish, more or less, that he caught and then lost. Young readers will be left to sort out fact from fantasy in this fun-loving story.

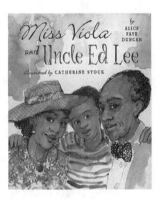

Miss Viola and Uncle Ed Lee [183]

Written by Alice Faye Duncan
Illustrated by Catherine Stock

Hardcover: Atheneum
Published 1999

Young Bradley is the unlikely matchmaker between his two senior citizen neighbors, Miss Viola and Uncle Ed Lee. Bradley has his work cut out for him, because even though Uncle Ed Lee would like to make friends with Miss Viola, the two are as opposite as night and day. Miss Viola is as neat and orderly as a pin, while Uncle Ed Lee is messy, disorderly, and sometimes even trifling. With Bradley's encouragement, Uncle Ed Lee cleans up his home and yard and successfully attracts Miss Viola.

Money Troubles [184]

Written by Bill Cosby
Illustrated by Varnette P. Honeywood

Hardcover and softcover: Cartwheel, Scholastic
Published 1998

Little Bill is determined to buy a telescope that costs $100, but he only has $47.87. Industriously, he washes and waxes neighbors' cars and collects soda cans in an attempt to earn the rest of the money. After he competes with another boy for empty soda cans in the park, he notices that the other boy obviously needs the money more than he does. With that realization, Little Bill sacrifices all of his cans to the other boy and donates his $47.87 to a food drive. This is a story of selflessness that may inspire young readers to see beyond themselves. Other books in the Little Bill series include: *The Best Way to Play* [95], *The Day I Saw My Father Cry* [117], *The Day I Was Rich* [118], *The Meanest Thing to Say* [180], *My Big Lie* [188], *One Dark and Scary Night* [206], *Shipwreck Sunday, Super-Fine Valentine* [237], *The Treasure Hunt* [241], and *The Worst Day of My Life* [257].

More Stories Huey Tells [185]

Written by Ann Cameron
Illustrated by Lis Toft

Hardcover: Farrar, Straus and Giroux
Published 1997

Young Huey relates five incredible stories from his eight-year-old perspective. In one story, "The Night I Turned Fifteen Billion," Huey decides that because the particles in the universe are fifteen billion years old, and since they have been recycled through the millennia, the particles in his body are fifteen billion years old, and therefore he is, too. There is a certain logic to his thinking on this subject and others that young readers will find amusing. This book is the sequel to the popular *The Stories Huey Tells* [230].

More Than Anything Else [186]

Written by Marie Bradby
Illustrated by Chris K. Soentpiet

Hardcover: Orchard, Grolier
Published 1996

Nine-year-old Booker T. Washington, who became the famous African American leader and educator, works in the salt mines of West Virginia with his father and brother. He has a burning desire to learn to read. In this fictionalized story, Booker's ambition is ignited when his mother gives him his first book. She is unable to read and so is he, but he is determined to learn. A local newspaper man, "a brown face of hope," helps Booker decipher the black marks on the pages and shows him how to write his name in the dirt. Booker's pure joy and optimism are evident in this richly illustrated book.

"I draw the marks on the dirt floor and try to figure out what sounds they make, what story their picture tells."

The Music in Derrick's Heart [187]

Written by Gwendolyn Battle-Lavert
Illustrated by Colin Bootman

Hardcover: Holiday
Published 2000

Young Derrick spends his entire summer taking harmonica lessons from his dear Uncle Booker T. Derrick spends his days listening to the sultry, soulful sounds that Uncle Booker T. makes on the mouth harp, and he goes to bed every night with the harmonica, trying to play his own music. Uncle Booker T. admonishes him to "slow down and take his time." Months later, after tenacious dedication, Booker blows a tune, from the heart, for his uncle.

My Big Lie [188]

Written by Bill Cosby
Illustrated by Varnette P. Honeywood

Hardcover and softcover: Cartwheel, Scholastic
Published 1999

Little Bill digs himself into a deep hole when he tries to avoid responsibility for a mistake by telling one little lie. The fabrication snowballs, requiring another lie and then another, until his story takes on a life of its own. Bill's story will remind young readers that one hard truth is better than a series of easy lies. Other books in the Little Bill series include *The Best Way to Play* [95], *The Day I Saw My Father Cry* [117], *The Day I Was Rich* [118], *The Meanest Thing to Say* [180], *Money Troubles* [184], *One Dark and Scary Night* [206], *Shipwreck Sunday, Super-Fine Valentine* [237], *The Treasure Hunt* [241], and *The Worst Day of My Life* [257].

My Dream of Martin Luther King [189]

Written and illustrated by Faith Ringgold

Hardcover: Crown
Published 1996

The author tells the story of Martin Luther King Jr. from the perspective of her own childhood dream. As her dream opens, she sees a world of people carrying bags full of prejudice, hate, ignorance, violence, and fear to exchange for bags of hope, freedom, peace, awareness, and love. Her dreams reflect real and imagined glimpses of the life of Martin Luther King Jr. to tell the story of his vision and civil rights leadership. By visualizing the story as the author tells it, young readers will be able to understand Dr. King's mission.

My Little Island [190]

Written and illustrated by Frané Lessac   ***Reading Rainbow* Feature Book**

Hardcover and softcover: HarperCollins
Published 1985

A young boy and his friend visit the Caribbean island of his birth. They meet new friends, eat delicious Caribbean food, take a drive, visit volcanoes, go to the market, and more. When the visit is over, they do not want to leave and agree to come back again soon.

My Mama Sings [191]

Written by Jeanne Whitehouse Peterson
Illustrated by Sandra Speidel

Hardcover: HarperCollins
Published 1994

A young boy is often entertained and comforted by the songs his mama sings to him. While she has no new songs, she does have a special song for every occasion—for bedtime, for doing the laundry, for playing in the leaves on a fall day. But one day, Mama has a terrible day and loses her job. She comes home with no songs at all. The loving young boy decides to cheer her up with his own self-composed ditty. Mama can't help but respond to his loving gesture.

> *"By myself I try singing all of Mama's old songs, but they don't sound the same. So I make up a song—a special song for Mama."*

My Man Blue [192]

Written by Nikki Grimes
Illustrated by Jerome Lagarrigue

Hardcover: Dial, Penguin Putnam
Published 1999

Fourteen artfully illustrated poems describe the relationship forged between a young boy, Damon, and his single mother's new boyfriend, Blue. Damon and Blue grow together, bonding in an endearing best friend, father-son-like relationship. The poetic chapters of their story include "Fearless," an expression of love and support from Blue to Damon, and "Like Blue," a tribute to Blue from Damon, who hopes to grow up like his role model.

Robert H.
Miller

<small>AUTHOR</small>

REFLECTIONS

"As a young boy growing up in the Pacific Northwest in the mid- to late 1950s, imitating white cowboy heroes from television and movies was a common occurrence. There were no children's books highlighting the exploits of African Americans in the settling of the wild, wild West and, for sure, no television episodes showcasing African American men as cowboys. Consequently, the books that interested me the most were adventure stories like *Peter Pan,* Grimm's fairy tales, and any story in which I could insert myself as the hero. Fortunately today, African American children clearly have an advantage over my generation."

OUR FAVORITES FROM
ROBERT H. MILLER

Buffalo Soldiers: The Story of Emanuel Stance [110]

A Pony for Jeremiah [323]

Reflections of a Black Cowboy: Pioneers [325]

The Story of Jean Baptiste DuSable [232]

My Mom Is My Show-and-Tell [193]

Written and illustrated by Dolores Johnson ☆ 72

Hardcover: Marshall Cavendish
Published 1999

Young David is a nervous wreck, worrying about his mother's appearance at his class's parent career day. As they walk to school together, David admonishes her to not call him Pumpkin, not hold his hand in front of his friends, not tell any silly jokes, and more. In spite of his early jitters, he proudly introduces his mother, his show-and-tell, when the time comes.

My Name Is York [194]

Written by Elizabeth Van Steenwyk
Illustrated by Bill Farnsworth

Hardcover: Rising Moon, Northland
Published 1997

"*Still, I dream, and I carry my dream within me as we begin our quest to find a waterway to the western sea. I dream of finding my freedom.*"

A little-known slave named York accompanied Captain Clark on the famous Lewis and Clark expedition in 1803. Although a slave, York stood side by side with Clark and experienced all of the adventure and thrill of their journey. The explorers encountered Indians, white-water rapids, snowy passages, and brilliant views of the northern lights. Yet what York really sought was his own freedom. This is a quiet story about the quests of both the historic expedition party and one solitary man.

My Rows and Piles of Coins [195]

Written by Tolowa M. Mollel
Illustrated by E. B. Lewis

Coretta Scott King Honor: Illustrator

Hardcover: Clarion
Published 1999

"*I emptied the box, arranged the coins in piles and the piles in rows. Then I counted the coins and thought about the blue and red bicycle.*"

An industrious young Tanzanian boy, Suruni, secretly saves the coins that his mother gives him every Saturday to spend at the marketplace. Instead of buying treats, Suruni saves to buy a new bike. He sorts, piles, and counts his savings every day, but his high hopes turn to disappointment when he realizes that he is still a long way from his goal. Even so, the virtuous young boy gets a bike from his supportive parents, who have known of the secret savings plan all along.

Nathaniel Talking [196]

Written by Eloise Greenfield ☆ 42
Illustrated by Jan Spivey Gilchrist

Coretta Scott King Award: Illustrator
Coretta Scott King Honor: Author

Hardcover: Black Butterfly, Writers & Readers
Published 1989

Warm black-and-white pencil drawings illustrate eighteen poetic raps from an exuberant nine-year-old. Nathaniel reflects on a broad range of subjects from the perspective of his young life, including "Making Friends," "My Daddy," "Nine," and "Knowledge."

NBA by the Numbers [197]

Written by Bruce Brooks
Photographs by the National Basketball Association

Hardcover: Scholastic
Published 1997

Young sports fans will be thrilled by the dynamic photographs of notable NBA players in action that dominate this book about the popular game. Descriptions of certain elements of the game, and the corresponding photographs, are arranged to count from one, as in "One Alert Dribbler" (in this case Scottie Pippin), to fifty, as in "The Fifty All-Time Stars," picturing the NBA's top players picked in commemoration of the association's fiftieth anniversary.

NBA Game Day: From Morning Until Night Behind the Scenes in the NBA [198]

Written by Joe Layden and James Preller
Photographs by Gary Gold

Hardcover: Scholastic
Published 1997

This photographic journal chronicles the lives of NBA players preparing for and playing their game. Candid color photographs reflect all aspects of the players' professional lives—from pregame preparation, practice, and game action to autograph signing. The text is minimal, but the pictures of many of the game's stars will tell the story for young fans.

A Net to Catch Time [199]

Written by Sara Harrell Banks
Illustrated by Scott Cook

Hardcover: Alfred A. Knopf
Published 1997

Young Cuffy is going crabbing with his father off the Georgia barrier islands, where they live. Young readers have a treat in store as they read this warm story about the young boy's fishing expedition—from first fowl crow (about 5:30 A.M.) until sundown (about 6:30 P.M.) and Cuffy's evening activities during Plat-eye Prowl (about 8:30 P.M. to midnight). The story is told in Cuffy's colorful Gullah language, especially the descriptive terms that mark the time of day. All the unfamiliar terms are nicely defined in a glossary. **Nonstandard English.**

The New King: A Madagascan Legend [200]

Adapted by Doreen Rappaport
Illustrated by E. B. Lewis

Hardcover: Dial, Penguin USA
Published 1995

A child, Prince Rakoto, suddenly becomes king when his beloved father dies in a hunting accident. His first act as king is to command that the royal doctors and magicians bring his father back to life, but they cannot. It takes the explanation of a wise woman to help Rakoto understand the circle of life and accept his father's death. This profound story with a tender message may be helpful in describing death to a young child.

Night Golf [201]

Written by William Miller
Illustrated by Cedric Lucas ☆ 88

Hardcover: Lee & Low
Published 1999

Young James finds his passion the day he discovers the game of golf. It is something he knows he can do, if only he is given the chance to play. But in the 1950s, golf was a game for "rich, white men," not for young black boys. So James becomes a caddy to be near the game he loves. He is befriended by an older, wiser caddy who invites him back to the course at night to play in the moonlight. James's story is a true representation of real events in African American sports history.

Nobiah's Well: A Modern African Folktale [202]

Written by Donna W. Guthrie
Illustrated by Rob Roth

Hardcover: Ideals Children's Books
Published 1993

Nobiah, a young African boy, embarks on a mission to fetch water for his family. Their village is parched, and the precious water is needed to drink and to water the few surviving plants that are their food. But on his way home, Nobiah gives in to his heart, offering the water to the thirsty hedgehog, hyena, and bear that he meets. To his mother's dismay, Nobiah's jar is empty by the time he arrives home. That night, the appreciative animals come to Nobiah's village and help him dig a well that is "as deep as his heart and as wide as his thirst."

Christopher Rand, age 6

"I really like *Christopher, Please Clean Up Your Room,* because the main character has my same name, but also because my mom is always telling me to clean up my room, too!"

O Christmas Tree [203]

Written by Vashanti Rahaman
Illustrated by Frané Lessac

Hardcover: Boyds Mills
Published 1996

Anslem is anxious to go to the docks to be first in line when the shipment of real Christmas trees comes to his Caribbean island. Disappointingly, only dried-up, good-for-nothing trees arrive. Anslem tries to paint and decorate the raggedy pines but fails to achieve his dream of having a real tree for the holiday. On Christmas morning a thoughtful neighbor helps Anslem recognize the real Christmas foliage in his own front yard. Bright, festive folk art illustrations of the Caribbean holiday frame the story.

The Old Cotton Blues [204]

Written by Linda England
Illustrated by Teresa Flavin

Hardcover: Margaret K. McElderry, Simon & Schuster
Published 1998

Young Dexter is enthralled by the riveting sound of Johnny Cotton's clarinet. Through the music Dexter can feel the "blue-down blues and the deep-down shaking, slow, laughing feel-goods." He wants to learn to play the clarinet himself, but his Mama cannot afford to buy him a clarinet. Johnny Cotton introduces Dexter to the harmonica, assuring him that, with a little practice, he will be able to express his blues just as well on the mouth harp. And later, Dexter does just that.

The Old, Old Man and the Very Little Boy [205]

Written by Kristine L. Franklin
Illustrated by Terea Shaffer

Hardcover: Atheneum Books for Young Readers, Simon & Schuster
Published 1992

As a young boy pays his daily respects to a village elder, he never imagines that he too will someday be old. The years pass, and the young boy becomes an old man receiving the same greetings from the village youth that he once gave to his elder. This is a tender book about the full cycle of life.

One Dark and Scary Night [206]

Written by Bill Cosby
Illustrated by Varnette P. Honeywood

Hardcover and softcover: Cartwheel, Scholastic
Published 1999

Little Bill faces the demons that are, at one time or another, in every child's room at bedtime. He sees strange flashes of light, hears threatening thumps, and just knows that something is in his closet. He runs to Mom and Dad for safety, but they return him to his bed. Then he runs to Alice the Great, his great-grandmother, who wisely uses a little child psychology to calm his shattered nerves. Other books in the Little Bill series include *The Best Way to Play* [95], *The Day I Saw My Father Cry* [117], *The Day I Was Rich* [118], *The Meanest Thing to Say* [180], *Money Troubles* [184], *My Big Lie* [188], *Shipwreck Sunday, Super-Fine Valentine* [237], *The Treasure Hunt* [241], and *The Worst Day of My Life* [257].

One Round Moon and a Star for Me [207]

Written by Ingrid Mennen
Illustrated by Niki Daly

Hardcover: Orchard
Published 1994

A young boy watches in amazement as his family celebrates the birth of his new sibling. His grandmother and aunts bring gifts for the baby. The village prepares to welcome their newest member. His father catches a falling star for his new child, whom he proudly declares as his own. Through it all the boy begins to question his place in the family and finally asks if he, too, is his father's child. In an endearing scene, Papa reassures the boy of his love and promises to catch a star for him, too.

> "*He puts his arms around me and says, 'Tonight, when the moon is big and round and the stars light up God's great sky, I'll show you, there is also a star for you.'*"

Walter

Dean

Myers

AUTHOR

REFLECTIONS

"I read a lot of comic books and any kind of thing I could find. One day, a teacher found me. She grabbed my comic book and tore it up. I was really upset, but then she brought in a pile of books from her own library. That was the best thing that ever happened to me. Books took me, not so much to foreign lands and fanciful adventures, but to a place within myself that I have been exploring ever since. The public library was my most treasured place. I couldn't believe my luck in discovering that what I enjoyed most—reading—was free."

OUR FAVORITES FROM
WALTER DEAN MYERS

The Journal of Joshua Loper: A Black Cowboy, The Chisholm Trail, 1871 [300]

Me, Mop, and the Moondance Kid [312]

Mouse Rap [315]

The Righteous Revenge of Artemis Bonner [326]

Smiffy Blue, Ace Crime Detective: The Case of the Missing Ruby and Other Stories [333]

Only a Pigeon [208]

Written by Christopher Kurtz and Jane Kurtz
Illustrated by E. B. Lewis

Hardcover: Simon & Schuster Books for Young Readers
Published 1997

A young boy, Ondu-ahlem, lives and works in virtual poverty in Ethiopia. His only joy is his small coop of pigeons, which he tends with great care, sometimes sleeping next to the coop to protect the birds and their eggs. One day, he and his friends play an all-or-nothing game with their prized pigeons. On a signal, two boys throw their birds into the air. The boy whose pigeon returns home, leading the other pigeon to his side, wins and gets to keep both birds. Young readers will gain a sense of the life and values of this young boy in modern Ethiopia. A photograph at the back of the book shows the Ethiopian boy who inspired this story, surrounded by his pigeons.

The Orphan Boy [209]

Written by Tololwa M. Mollel
Illustrated by Paul Morin

Hardcover and softcover: Clarion, Houghton Mifflin
Published 1991

A star from the sky, named Kilekan, comes to earth embodied as a small boy to be a companion and son to an old man. Kilekan brings extraordinarily good luck to the old man by using celestial powers that he must keep secret. The old man becomes so curious that he breaks his trust with the boy in order to discover the secret, forcing Kilekan to return to his place in the sky. This gentle story, illustrated with intricate paintings, establishes how the Maasai people came to refer to the planet Venus as Kilekan, the orphan boy.

Over the Green Hills [210]

Written and illustrated by Rachel Isadora

Hardcover: Greenwillow, William Morrow
Published 1992

Young Zolani and his mother journey across the South African countryside to visit Grandmother. Along the way, the two stop to shop, help a distressed neighbor, and rest by the roadside. Disappointingly, Grandmother is not at home when they arrive. The two wait patiently until they finally see Grandmother coming down the road. Authentic landscapes of the South African countryside and scenes of rural village life support the simple story line.

The Paperboy [211]

Written and illustrated by Dav Pilkey   Caldecott Honor Book

Hardcover: Orchard
Published 1996

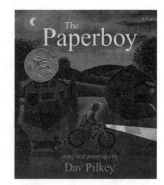

In the wee hours of the morning, while it is still dark outside and everyone is still asleep, a responsible young boy arises with his faithful dog to prepare for his paper route. In beautifully illustrated night scenes, he rides through his well-practiced route, delivering papers while the dog follows behind. He returns home just as everyone else is getting up and goes back to bed to finish his night's sleep.

A Picture Book of Thurgood Marshall [212]

Written by David A. Adler
Illustrated by Robert Casilla

Hardcover: Holiday
Published 1997

This elementary-level biography tells the compelling story of Thurgood Marshall, who was taught by his dedicated parents to value a good education and to work hard. Armed with a Lincoln University education and a willingness to apply himself, young Marshall became an attorney and then the chief counsel for the NAACP. Marshall made a career of challenging racial discrimination, hallmarked by his legal victory in the Brown v. Board of Education case that forced school desegregation. Marshall, who became known as Mr. Civil Rights, defied all odds by becoming the first African American Supreme Court justice in history. Other subjects of the Picture Book Biography series include Frederick Douglass, Jackie Robinson, Jesse Owens, and Martin Luther King Jr.

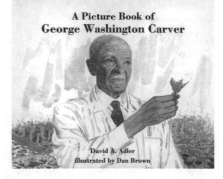

Playing Games [213]

Written by Donna Jo Napoli
Illustrations by Lauren Klementz-Harte

Softcover: Aladdin, Simon & Schuster
Published 2000

The Little Angel of Imagination receives the important assignment of inspiring young Louis, down on earth, to play creatively with his younger brother. Louis, a couch potato, would rather watch television than be bothered with the small child. Little Angel perceives, correctly, that all Louis lacks is imaginativeness, so he focuses his angelic powers, dabbling in Louis's life, to stimulate his underactive imagination. This entertaining, easy-to-read chapter book is one in the Angelwings series, in which a cast of angels watch over and help earthly children.

Poppa's Itchy Christmas [214]

Written by Angela Shelf Medearis
Illustrated by John Ward

Hardcover: Holiday
Published 1998

Young George can hardly contain his disappointment when both he and Poppa each receive an ugly knit muffler and a pair of bright red, itchy long johns for Christmas. His only satisfying gift is a pair of new ice skates. When George goes to try out the new skates, he falls through the cracked ice and almost perishes until he is rescued by Poppa, who ingeniously uses the knit muffler to pull George to safety. Poppa, Big Mama, Grandma Tiny, and Aunt Viney are all reprised characters in this winsome sequel to *Poppa's New Pants* [215].

Poppa's New Pants [215]

"I pried my eyes and slowly looked around the room. A big, white ghost was drifting through the doorway, and it was coming toward me!"

Written by Angela Shelf Medearis
Illustrated by John Ward

Hardcover: Holiday
Published 1995

In a comedy of errors, Poppa's new pants, which were originally six inches too long, are cut off above the knee when each of the three women in the house, unbeknownst to one another, decides to surprise him by cutting and hemming the pants. The young son, an unknowing witness to the nighttime escapades, mistakes the three do-gooders for ghosts, adding a humorous subplot to the story. The sequel to this entertaining story is *Poppa's Itchy Christmas* [214].

Read for Me, Mama [216]

Written by Vashanti Rahaman
Illustrated by Lori McElrath-Eslick

Hardcover: Boyds Mills
Published 1997

This sensitive story about a hard-working single mother and her loving son will touch young readers. Joseph loves to read and checks two books out of the library—one that he can read by himself and another, more difficult one for his Mama to read to him. But every day Mama has a reason to avoid reading. On Mondays there was grocery shopping to do; on Tuesdays, housecleaning; on Wednesdays, choir practice; on Thursdays, laundry. And on Fridays Mama claimed to be too tired. Joseph finally learns in a dramatic climax that Mama cannot read. But she is eager to learn, and Joseph is more than happy to support her efforts.

The Real McCoy: The Life of an African American Inventor [217]

Written by Wendy Towle
Illustrated by Wil Clay

Softcover: Scholastic
Published 1993

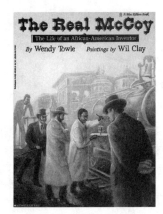

Young readers will be inspired by knowing that Elijah McCoy, a free-born black man from Canada, was a premier engineer and inventor back in the mid-1800s. McCoy invented many things, for which he received little historical credit. Most noteworthy of his inventions was an oil drip cup that revolutionized the locomotive industry. Many others tried to develop better versions of the oil cup, but McCoy's original was always superior, which gave rise to the phrase "the real McCoy."

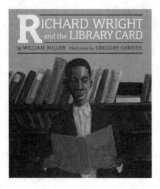

Richard Wright and the Library Card [218]

Written by William Miller
Illustrated by Gregory Christie

Hardcover: Lee & Low
Published 1997

Richard Wright, a young black boy in Mississippi in 1908, yearned to learn to read. In this fictionalized account of the famous writer's early days, he did learn and was on a constant quest for more reading material. He devoured everything he could, but as a black person in the old South, he was denied access to the library. Richard was befriended by his white employer, Mr. Falk, who understood Richard's hunger for books and allowed Richard to use his library card. Of course, they both had to pretend that the books Richard checked out were for Mr. Falk. Richard continued to be inspired by what he read until he was able to write his own novels. In 1940, his novel *Native Son* was published, followed by his autobiography, the acclaimed *Black Boy*, in 1945.

Robert Lives with His Grandparents [219]

Written by Martha Whitmore Hickman
Illustrated by Tim Hinton

Hardcover: Albert Whitman
Published 1995

After his parents' divorce, and because of his mother's drug problem, Robert comes to live with his grandparents. He loves and appreciates his grandparents but is embarrassed to admit that he does not live with his own parents. When his grandparents come to school for an open house, Robert is forced to admit his living arrangement. He is pleased and surprised to find out that he is not alone. Everyone is very positive about the situation, which is excellent reinforcement for children who live in nontraditional family situations.

Sam and the Tigers: A New Retelling of Little Black Sambo [220]

Written by Julius Lester ☆ 80
Illustrated by Jerry Pinkney

Hardcover: Dial
Published 1996

The story of Little Black Sambo is retold in this entertaining and politically correct version. The offensive racial stereotypes of the original story are gone, and what is left is the humorous tale of a young boy, Sam, who lives in the town of Sam-sam-sa-mara with his mother and father, both also named Sam. Sam the boy comes face to face with a group of tigers and is forced to give them his hip new suit of clothes in exchange for his life. But the clever boy finds a way to outsmart the not-so-smart tigers. It may seem that there are too many Sams in this engaging story, but young readers will love reading it to the delightful end.

> "*There was a little boy in Sam-sam-sa-mara named Sam. Sam's mama was also named Sam. So was Sam's Daddy. In fact, all the people in Sam-sam-sa-mara were named Sam.*"

Satchmo's Blues [221]

Written by Alan Schroeder
Illustrated by Floyd Cooper

Hardcover: Doubleday
Published 1996

In this fictionalized biography, young Louis Armstrong dreams of becoming a musician and tries to save five dollars to buy the horn that he has seen in a pawnshop window. Just before he achieves his goal, Louis experiences a disappointing financial setback. In spite of that, he goes on to buy the trumpet and to become the most famous trumpeter of his time. The moral of the story is that goal-setting, hard work, determination, and the universal truth that nothing worth having comes easily are the keys to success.

Sebgugugu the Glutton: A Bantu Tale from Rwanda, Africa [222]

Written by Verna Aardema
Illustrated by Nancy L. Clouse

Hardcover: Africa World
Published 1993

Sebgugugu is a very poor man who calls upon Imana, the Lord of Rwanda, to help provide for his family. Imana responds kindly on several occasions, providing a bounty of food for Sebgugugu and his family. Each time, Imana cautions Sebgugugu about what he must do to protect the endowment, but greed always makes the foolish man risk what he has for what he thinks will bring more. Strong cut-paper collages embellish this African folktale.

THE CREATOR'S

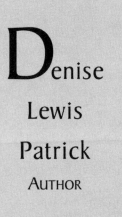

D enise

Lewis

Patrick

AUTHOR

REFLECTIONS

"My favorite stories as a young child were fairy tales, the classic Grimm Brothers and Hans Christian Andersen ones. I loved the magical fantasy aspects of these stories— kings, queens, fairies, scary witches, and sorcerers. It would have been wonderful for me to have read books like *Mufaro's Beautiful Daughters* or *The People Could Fly*. It would have been amazing to know as a small child that my face, my history, my ancestors could be woven into the same magic that intrigued me. I would have been living at the public library!"

OUR FAVORITES FROM
DENISE LEWIS PATRICK

Adventures of Midnight Son [263]

I Can Count [40]

The Longest Ride [309]

Senefer: A Young Genius in Old Egypt [223]

Written by Beatrice Lumpkin
Illustrated by Linda Nickens

Softcover: Africa World
Published 1992

Ancient Egyptian base-ten counting principles, which are the basis of modern mathematics, are ingeniously embedded in this story of a young Egyptian boy, Senefer, who grew up to become a famous mathematician and engineer in this early enlightened civilization. Young readers may embrace the principles illustrated in several counting, equation, and word problems found throughout the story. Additionally, the science of mathematics is correctly credited to African people.

Shaq and the Beanstalk: And Other Very Tall Tales [224]

Written by Shaquille O'Neal
Illustrated by Shane W. Evans

Hardcover: Cartwheel, Scholastic
Published 1999

NBA star turned story-teller Shaquille O'Neal serves up six well-known fairy tales with his own twist. In each of the fun-loving fractured tales, such as "Shaq and the Beanstalk" and "Shaq and the Three Bears," Shaq himself takes the leading role. The stories are told with plenty of hip language, and many of the colorful illustrations contain the sports hero's likeness. Young basketball fans won't mind this digression into early childhood fairy tales with Shaq as their guide.

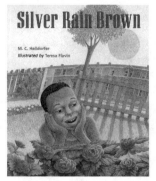

Silver Rain Brown [225]

Written by M. C. Helldorfer
Illustrated by Teresa Flavin

Hardcover: Houghton Mifflin
Published 1999

An expectant mother and her son endure a summer heat wave. It is so hot and water is so scarce that they can't even use water to wash cars or water the flowers. Momma's new baby is born the night that it finally rains, cooling the neighborhood and watering the earth. The new baby is appropriately named Silver Rain, a name descriptive of the rain that fell on the night of her birth.

The Singing Man: Adapted from a West African Folktale [226]

Adapted by Angela Shelf Medearis
Illustrated by Terea Shaffer

Coretta Scott King Honor: Illustrator

Hardcover and softcover: Holiday
Published 1994

In the West African city of Lagos, a young man must declare his career plans when he is initiated into manhood. In this sophisticated story, when Banzar declares that he will become a musician, he is banished from the village for choosing such an unproductive vocation. Over the years, Banzar becomes a very famous singer, intoning songs about the history and heritage of his people. He returns home many years later and is welcomed and honored for his accomplishment.

> "*Banzar put on his finest robe. He filled his bags with food, gifts, and money, and called his servants. They went before Banzar into the village of his boyhood, beating drums and gongs and calling out, 'Make way for the musician of the king of Lagos.'*"

Somebody's New Pajamas [227]

Written by Isaac Jackson
Illustrated by David Soman

Hardcover: Dial, Penguin USA
Published 1996

The lifestyle differences between Jerome and his friend Robert are obvious when Jerome spends the night with Robert. Robert has soft, comfortable pajamas, but Jerome does not, because his family has never been able to afford such luxuries. Jerome wants a pair of new pajamas, too, until he recognizes that the pajamas are not as important as the pride that he has in his family.

Somewhere in Africa [228]

Written by Ingrid Mennen and Niki Daly
Illustrated by Nicolaas Maritz

Softcover: Puffin Unicorn, Puffin
Published 1992

A young boy named Ashraf lives in Africa, but not the Africa that might come to mind when young readers think about that continent. Ashraf's home is a big city teeming with skyscrapers, bustling with cars, and alive with the energy of any large metropolitan area. Ashraf's only view of the wilder side of Africa comes from books, whose pictures of lions, zebras, and crocodiles fascinate him. Your young reader's vision of Africa will broaden with the new knowledge that Africa has more than jungles and wild animals.

Stevie [229]

Written and illustrated by John Steptoe

Hardcover: Harper & Row
Published 1969

During the week, while his mother works, little Stevie comes to stay with Robert and his family. Robert finds the situation totally hopeless. The younger Stevie plays with all of Robert's toys, messes up his bed, and generally makes a pest of himself. Young readers will be convinced that there is nothing good about having Stevie around until the care-giving arrangement comes to an end, and then Robert reminisces about the good times that he and Stevie shared. **Nonstandard English.**

The Stories Huey Tells [230]

Written by Ann Cameron
Illustrated by Roberta Smith

Hardcover: Knopf, Random House
Published 1995

"*The giant mush-rooms were all around the plate, just like a forest. The trout was in the middle. . . . His eye was big and white and sad and cooked. It looked right straight at me."*

Huey is the younger brother of the well-known Julian, of *Julian's Glorious Summer* [160] and other books. In this book, Huey relates five stories from his young experiences, all engagingly told from a kid's point of view. Our favorite was "The Rule." In Huey's family, everyone must try everything on their plate and must eat everything that they order in a restaurant. That is a double whammy for Huey when he orders trout (head and tail intact) and mushrooms for dinner. Young readers will empathize with Huey, and you will chuckle imagining your own eight-year-old trying to contend with this dilemma. The sequel is *More Stories Huey Tells* [185].

Storm in the Night [231]

Written by Mary Stolz   **Coretta Scott King Honor: Illustrator**
Illustrated by Pat Cummings

Hardcover and softcover: HarperCollins
Published 1988

When a grandfather and grandson are caught in a darkened house during a stormy night, an intimate evening of appreciation is shared between the two. There are several other books about Thomas and his grandfather: *Go Fish* [293], *Stealing Home* [336], and *Coco Grimes*.

The Story of Jean Baptiste DuSable [232]

Written by Robert H. Miller ☆ 104
Illustrated by Richard Leonard

Hardcover: Silver, Paramount
Published 1995

Jean Baptiste DuSable, a black Frenchman who immigrated to North America, is fully credited in this simply told story as the founder of Eschikagoo, a prosperous trading post on the banks of Lake Michigan in 1772. What young readers will not understand until they read the entire story is that the city DuSable established is now known as Chicago. Other books in the series include *Buffalo Soldiers: The Story of Emanuel Stance* [110] and *The Story of Nat Love.*

A Strawbeater's Thanksgiving [233]

Written by Irene Smalls ☆ 160
Illustrated by Melodye Benson Rosales

Hardcover: Little, Brown
Published 1998

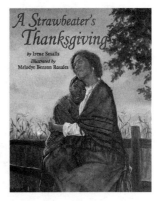

Traditionally, during the harvest time in late November, slaves were permitted to celebrate the end of their work. The gaiety would include corn-husking contests, singing, dancing, and other frivolities. One year, seven-year-old Jess decides that he is old enough to serve as the "strawbeater," the boy who stands behind the fiddler and reaches around to beat the fiddle strings while the fiddler plays. But Jess would have to wrestle the much older, much larger Nathaniel for that honor. The vivid and expressive illustrations put young readers in the middle of the action of this lively story. **Nonstandard English.**

Strong to the Hoop [234]

Written by John Coy
Illustrated by Leslie Jean-Bart

Hardcover: Lee & Low
Published 1999

James's time has finally come. He has always had to watch his older brother play basketball from the sidelines, but now one of the players is injured and James is called in to play. James is smaller and younger, but he has everything to prove in this high-stakes neighborhood game. His determination and raw energy are evident in the description of the play-by-play action. The text is street real, and the action is captured in snapshot illustrations.

Dennis Collins, reading to his twins, Charles and Lionel, age 2, says of his two restless sons, "They really like any book I read as long as it doesn't take more than ten minutes to read."

Summer Wheels [235]

Written by Eve Bunting
Illustrated by Thomas B. Allen

Softcover: Voyager, Harcourt Brace
Published 1992

The good-hearted Bicycle Man fixes up bikes and allows the neighborhood kids to ride them. There were only a few rules that the kids had to live by. The first was that bikes be returned by four o'clock and the second was that the kids were responsible for fixing any damage to the bikes they rode. Most of the neighborhood kids respected the rules, especially Brady and his friend. But when a new boy, Leon, comes and blatantly disregards the rules, the two veterans take matters into their own hands. Twice they deliver Leon and his missing bikes to Bicycle Man, but they cannot understand why Bicycle Man continues to extend his kindness to the errant boy. The wise Bicycle Man seems to understand that Leon is crying out for attention and support, which he is more than willing to extend.

Sundiata: Lion King of Mali [236]

Written by David Wisniewski
Illustrated by Lee Salsbery

Hardcover: Clarion
Published 1992

Bright cut-paper illustrations help add drama to this African story of deceit and political intrigue. Sundiata, who was both lame and mute, was named heir to his father's throne in the great empire of Mali. But when the time came for Sundiata to ascend to the throne, the council of elders passed him over in favor of his older half-brother. Over time, the weak half-brother lost the empire to an evil sorcerer king, who brought the great empire to ruin. While in exile, Sundiata rose to the challenge of saving his nation. He gained not only his voice, but the physical strength and cunning necessary to conquer his enemy and restore his homeland to its former greatness.

Super-Fine Valentine [237]

Written by Bill Cosby
Illustrated by Varnette P. Honeywood

Hardcover and softcover: Cartwheel, Scholastic
Published 1998

In a typical third-grade experience, Little Bill is insecure and shy about his crush on Mia. His friends have noticed that he likes her and teased him about it, and his brother has exposed Little Bill's feelings to their parents. Now it is Valentine's Day and Little Bill has to decide whether or not to give Mia the card that he has made especially for her. After a wrenching process, Little Bill finally gives her the card and decides that it is best to show people you like them. Other books in the Little Bill series include *The Best Way to Play* [95], *The Day I Saw My Father Cry* [117], *The Day I Was Rich* [118], *The Meanest Thing to Say* [180], *Money Troubles* [184], *My Big Lie* [188], *One Dark and Scary Night* [206], *Shipwreck Sunday*, *The Treasure Hunt* [241], and *The Worst Day of My Life* [257].

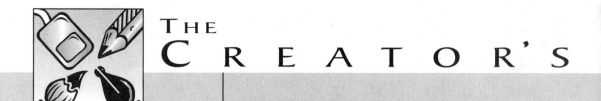

THE CREATOR'S

Harriette Gillem Robinet

AUTHOR

"My mother read *Three Little Pigs* and Grimm fairy tales along with Bible stories to me. I read *Heidi, Black Beauty, Little Women, Little Men,* and *Hitty's First One Hundred Years* myself. I had no image of African American children as a part of American society.

"Therefore it is important to provide historical and contemporary fiction that places black children as *heroes* in American society *along with* other races."

OUR FAVORITES FROM
HARRIETTE GILLEM ROBINET

Tailypo! [238]

Retold by Jan Wahl
Illustrated by Wil Clay

Hardcover: Henry Holt
Published 1991

An old man who lives alone in the woods strikes out at a creature that he finds in his cabin. He cuts off the creature's tail and eats it for dinner. But the creature retaliates by returning time and time again, demanding the return of his "tailypo." Each time the old man sends his dogs to chase the creature away. Eventually, the creature confronts the old man and devours him to get back the tailypo. The tale is fast-paced and intriguing, but suitable only for young readers who can handle the dark story line.

Teammates [239]

Written by Peter Golenbock
Illustrated by Paul Bacon

Hardcover and softcover: Gulliver, Harcourt Brace
Published 1990

This excellent easy-to-read book tells the true story of the integration of major league baseball by Jackie Robinson. A young child can easily understand the integration strategy of Branch Rickey, the humiliation of Jackie Robinson, and the compassion of Pee Wee Reese, the white player who finally embraced Robinson on the field, both figuratively and literally. Photographs of the key characters are interspersed with illustrations that support the story.

Tommy Traveler in the World of Black History [240]

Written and illustrated by Tom Feelings ☆ 36

Hardcover and softcover: Black Butterfly, Writers & Readers
Published 1991

Tommy is unable to find books about black history in his public library, so he visits a doctor who has a private collection of books on the subject. As Tommy reads, he falls asleep and dreams that he is actually part of the historical stories of Phoebe Fraunces, Emmet Till, Aesop, Frederick Douglass, Crispus Attucks, and Joe Louis. The story is presented in a comic-book style that will attract and engage many young readers.

The Treasure Hunt [241]

Written by Bill Cosby
Illustrated by Varnette P. Honeywood

Hardcover and softcover: Cartwheel, Scholastic
Published 1997

Little Bill is in a quandary after he realizes that he has no special treasure. His father is engrossed in his album collection. His mother seems to care a great deal about her china, and his brother is into his baseball card collection. While Bill is in his room looking for his own treasure, his Great-Grandmother Alice comes in and wisely prods Little Bill to tell her a story. He makes up an incredibly creative and funny story that makes Great-Grandmother laugh. In the process he realizes his own treasure—storytelling. Other books in the Little Bill series include *The Best Way to Play* [95], *The Day I Saw My Father Cry* [117], *The Day I Was Rich* [118], *The Meanest Thing to Say* [180], *Money Troubles* [184], *My Big Lie* [188], *One Dark and Scary Night* [206], *Shipwreck Sunday, Super-Fine Valentine* [237], and *The Worst Day of My Life* [257].

> **"M**y treasure hunt is over. I learned what was special to me—telling stories and making people laugh. . . . You can't polish or dust or sort my special things. You can only enjoy them."

Trouble [242]

Written by Jane Kurtz
Illustrated by Durga Bernhard

Hardcover: Gulliver, Harcourt Brace
Published 1997

A young Ethiopian boy always seems to find himself in the line of trouble, no matter what he does. Teklah's father makes him a game board, hoping to help occupy him while he tends the family's goats, so that he cannot get into trouble. Uncannily, however, Teklah gets involved in a series of troubled encounters that result in his losing the game board. In this witty story, things go full circle and Teklah manages to get a new game board at the end of the day.

Two and Too Much [243]

Written by Mildred Pitts Walter ☆ 174
Illustrated by Pat Cummings

Hardcover: Bradbury, Macmillan
Published 1990

Seven-year-old Brandon has his hands full when he agrees to watch his two-year-old sister, Gina, while his mother does the housework. Gina is everything two-year-olds are reputed to be—too busy, too uncooperative, and much too negative. Her favorite word, of course, is "No!," which challenges young Brandon's patience as a big brother.

Ty's One-Man Band [244]

Written by Mildred Pitts Walter ☆ 174
Illustrated by Margot Tomes

Reading Rainbow Review Book

Softcover: Scholastic
Published 1980

"*Boys and girls, mothers and fathers, even the babies clapped their hands. Some danced in the street. Whenever the music stopped, everybody shouted, 'More.'*"

Young Ty meets an intriguing stranger, a one-legged man who claims he is a one-man band. At the stranger's bidding, Ty collects a washboard, two wooden spoons, a tin pail, and a comb from his dubious family members, promising them a concert in return. Late in the evening the stranger shows up and keeps his promise, to the enjoyment of the entire community. Then, just as mysteriously as he came, the stranger disappears back into the night.

Vacation in the Village: A Story from West Africa [245]

Written and illustrated by Pierre Yves Njeng

Softcover: Boyds Mills
Published 1999

Young Nwemb is skeptical about his family's summer vacation to a village outside their city. Concerned that he will be bored in the country, away from city life and without his friends, Nwemb boards the train for the journey. Despite his worries, Nwemb finds a new friend and a summer full of fun in the village and looks forward to his next visit.

The Wagon [246]

Written by Tony Johnston
Illustrated by James E. Ransome

Hardcover: Tambourine, William Morrow
Published 1996

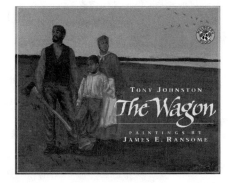

A young slave boy has ambivalent feelings about the wagon that
he and his father built for their master in this provocative story
book. The wagon is both a tangible emblem of his enslavement
and the vehicle that can carry him to the freedom that he craves.

Wagon Wheels [247]

Written by Barbara Brenner
Illustrated by Don Bolognese

Reading Rainbow Review Book

Hardcover and softcover: HarperCollins
Published 1993

The incredible story of the Muldie boys and their father is told in this easy-to-
read book of historical fiction. The boys—ages eleven, eight, and three—move
with their father to Kansas and are then left alone for months while he goes
on to find a better homestead. The boys live alone in a hole carved in the
ground and care for one another under incredibly difficult circumstances,
including a prairie fire that sweeps across their subterranean home. When
their father sends word that he is settled, along with a rough map, the three
young children travel alone for over 150 miles to reunite with him.

> "*There is a map with this letter. The map shows where I am and where you are. Follow the map. . . . You will find me. I know you can do it because you are my fine big boys.*"

A Weed Is a Flower: The Life of George Washington Carver [248]

Written and illustrated by Aliki

Softcover: Aladdin, Simon & Schuster
Published 1988

Born a poor, sickly slave, George Washington Carver was a special child who
took every opportunity to learn and to attend school. He grew up to be one of
the most important agriculturists in American history. His work distinguished
him among his peers and dramatically changed farming practices in this country. This version of Carver's life is presented at a primary level, so even the
youngest readers can understand his achievements.

What Kind of Baby-Sitter Is This? [249]

Written and illustrated by Dolores Johnson ☆ 72

Hardcover: Macmillan
Published 1991

Kevin can tell with one look that he is in for one of those evenings when Mrs. Pritchard comes to baby-sit. But, to his surprise, Mrs. Pritchard tunes in to a baseball game and seems to know everything about the sport. Hmh! Maybe the evening will be okay! Like Kevin, young readers will learn that it is not wise to judge a book by its cover.

What's So Funny, Ketu? [250]

Written by Verna Aardema
Illustrated by Marc Brown

Hardcover: Dial
Published 1982

An African villager, Ketu, rescues a small snake and is rewarded with a special gift or a curse, depending upon how you look at it. Ketu has been given the ability to hear the thoughts of animals but is forbidden, under threat of death, to tell anybody else about his new talent. Ketu overhears the thoughts of a mosquito, a rat, and a cow, which sends him into fits of laughter. Nobody, especially his frustrated wife, understands Ketu's odd behavior. The village elders are finally called upon to judge Ketu's actions, forcing him to divulge his secret, and to face death. An unexpected twist in the story saves Ketu's life and will bring a giggle to young readers.

When I Was Little [251]

Written by Toyomi Igus
Illustrated by Higgins Bond

Hardcover and softcover: Just Us
Published 1992

Young Noel and his grandfather spend a day fishing in this soulful book. The two engage in a very believable conversation about the differences between now and when Grandfather was a child. Grandfather explains to the incredulous Noel that there were no indoor toilets, televisions, VCRs, jet airplanes, or washing machines when he was a boy. The illustrations come to life in exquisite color, except the pictures of Grandfather's memories, which are presented in black and white for a striking visual effect.

Wiley and the Hairy Man [252]

Retold by Judy Sierra
Illustrated by Brian Pinkney

Hardcover: Lodestar, Dutton
Published 1996

In this African American folktale from Alabama, young Wiley encounters the frightening Hairy Man, who is known to gobble up young children. Wiley keeps his cool and uses his wits to outsmart the beast and escape. Having done so once, all Wiley has to do is outsmart Hairy Man two more times and the monster will never bother him again. The second time Wiley and the creature meet, he tricks Hairy Man into using his own conjurer talents against himself. Young readers will enjoy this suspenseful tale and the creative trick that Wiley uses in his third and final encounter with Hairy Man.

William and the Good Old Days [253]

Written by Eloise Greenfield ☆ 42
Illustrated by Jan Spivey Gilchrist

Hardcover: HarperCollins
Published 1993

In this sensitive exploration of a child's innermost feelings, young William yearns for his grandmother's recovery after her extended illness. He reminisces about their wonderful times together and looks forward to the return of the good old days.

> "*But yesterday, when Mommy and Daddy took me to her house, her face looked real tired, so I kissed it softly and hugged her, but not too tight.*"

Willie Jerome [254]

Written by Alice Faye Duncan
Illustrated by Tyrone Geter

Hardcover: Macmillan
Published 1995

Willie Jerome is always on the roof, blowin' his cool jazz sounds throughout his urban neighborhood. His young sister Judy loves the "sizzlin' red hot beebop" that Jerome plays, but nobody else does. His mother, friends, and other neighbors say that Jerome has no talent and that his music is only noise. Finally, Judy, acting as an advocate for her brother, convinces Mama to really tune in and listen to Jerome. Mama does and appreciates his music for the first time. **Nonstandard English.**

> "*So Mama loosens up her frown and takes a seat by me on the stoop. We close our eyes. We rest our minds and let the music speak.*"

Willie's Not the Hugging Kind [255]

Written by Joyce Durham Barrett
Illustrated by Pat Cummings

Hardcover and softcover: HarperCollins
Published 1989

Young Willie gives up hugging his mom and dad, feeling that he is too old for such nonsense. But soon starts to miss the warmth and security of those reassuring hugs. He finally realizes that he still needs the embrace of those he loves and those who love him. Leave this book around to help your remote young readers understand that demonstrative family affection has a place.

Wood-Hoopoe Willie [256]

Written by Virginia Kroll
Illustrated by Katherine Roundtree

Hardcover and softcover: Charlesbridge
Published 1993

Willie, who loves music, is constantly tapping out rhythms—with chopsticks at the Chinese restaurant, with pencils at school, and on tabletops with forks and knives. Everywhere Willie goes, he finds something to get the beat going. Willie's grandfather muses that Willie has a wood-hoopoe, an African pecking bird, trapped within him and teaches Willie about African instrumentation. The family goes to a Kwanzaa festival, where Willie gets the unexpected opportunity to sit in for a missing drummer, releasing his wood-hoopoe talents. The vibrancy of the story is matched by the intensely colored Afrocentric paintings.

The Worst Day of My Life [257]

Written by Bill Cosby
Illustrated by Varnette P. Honeywood

Hardcover and softcover: Scholastic
Published 1999

Little Bill cannot believe what is happening to his home. A huge tent has been raised in the yard; his usually clean home is even cleaner; his badminton net and basketball hoop were taken down; flowers and fancy platters of food appear; and now his mother wants him to put on his best clothes. Not just his good T-shirt, but a suit and tie. Bill's parents are having a party and Bill does not look forward to dozens of strange adults telling him how much he has grown. But Bill is a good son and a good sport who cooperates with his anxious parents, even though it may well be the worst day of his life. Other books in the Little Bill series include *The Best Way to Play* [95], *The Day I Saw My Father Cry* [117], *The Day I Was Rich* [118], *The Meanest Thing to Say* [180], *Money Troubles* [184], *My Big Lie* [188], *One Dark and Scary Night* [206], *Shipwreck Sunday, Super-Fine Valentine* [237], and *The Treasure Hunt* [241].

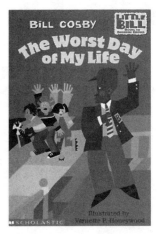

Your Dad Was Just Like You [258]

Written and illustrated by Dolores Johnson ☆ 72

Hardcover: Macmillan
Published 1993

Young Peter and his father are at odds with each other in this earnest story. Dad does not feel that Peter is serious enough about his schoolwork. To make matters worse, Peter has just carelessly broken an old cup on Dad's dresser. Peter cries to his grandfather, who then relates a compelling story about Dad when he was a boy, apparently very much like Peter at the same age. He also explains the significance of the old cup. The story helps Peter to better understand his father and motivates him to try to develop a more positive relationship with his dad.

> " *Y*ou see, when your father was a boy, he and I used to fight a lot. . . . We decided to change what was wrong between us. That day, we became a real serious father and son."

Your Move [259]

Written by Eve Bunting
Illustrated by James Ransome

Hardcover: Harcourt Brace
Published 1998

Ten-year-old James so desperately wants to belong to the K-Bones Club that he sneaks out with his younger brother to impress the would-be friends. They say they aren't a gang, yet as a rite of passage the K-Bones engage in the "take-it" game (stealing). They also force James to provoke their rival club, the Snakes, by spray-painting over their insignia, which results in a shoot-out that endangers both James and his younger brother. James is forced to face reality and to make the choice between acceptance by this trouble-making group and standing up for his values.

Zamani Goes to Market [260]

Written by Muriel Feelings
Illustrated by Tom Feelings ☆ 36

Hardcover: Africa World
Published 1990

Young Zamani experiences one of the passages into adulthood when he is allowed, for the first time, to accompany his father and brother to market. Zamani's wide-eyed enthusiasm for every aspect of the excursion is pleasing. Moreover, Zamani selflessly takes his own money to buy a special gift for his mother. His kindness is a reflection of the way he was raised, a point that becomes obvious in the telling of this touching story.

Books for
Middle Readers

THE MOST EXCITING thing about the ninety selections in this section is that you may enjoy them as much as your young son or student. There are a number of powerful stories ranging from inspirational biographies and compelling stories of slavery and emancipation to books of poetry, sports, and adventure. Even as we read and reviewed them, we were enlightened, engaged, and intrigued by many of the selections.

Books based on adolescent situations tend to be very popular with young boys. Identifying with the characters in the novels is reinforcing to the developing preteen, who may not understand that his feelings and reactions are shared by other young people.

Several books, such as *Anthony's Big Surprise* [266], *Chevrolet Saturdays* [275], and *Darnell Rock Reporting* [277], are about realistically based situations ranging from school and friendship dilemmas to family challenges. The characters are black, which may help African American boys relate to them, but their hurdles can easily apply to any adolescent boy.

There is a wonderful selection of books of historical fiction (or fictionalized stories based on real-life characters) that offer illuminating views of African American history. *The Captive* [274], *Ajeemah and His Son* [264], and *Silent Thunder: A Civil War Story* [330] are riveting accounts of slavery. *Forty Acres and Maybe a Mule* [287]; *The Journal of Joshua Loper: A Black Cowboy, The Chisolm Trail, 1871* [300]; and *The Longest Ride* [309] offer insight into the lives of some ex-slaves after emancipation, telling the stories of young black men caught up in slavery and its aftermath without being diminished by the experience. Books such as *Mississippi Chariot* [314] and *The Friendship* [290] depict the continuing effects of racism as recently as the mid-twentieth century. Empathetic young readers will easily recognize the character and dignity of the characters and take pride in their strength.

This chapter is chock-full of books about African American men who achieved and contributed remarkably, despite the oppression of racism, in a variety of fields from sports to whaling. *Black Hands, White Sails: The Story of African-American Whalers* [270] and *Sink or Swim: African-American Lifesavers of the Outer Banks* [331] are about the unsung African Americans who were early whalers and sea service men. *Black Diamond: The Story of the Negro Baseball Leagues* [269] and *Black Hoops: The History of African Americans in Basketball* [271] herald the early stories of blacks in two popular American sports.

As your son or student continues to grow and mature, he will need a steady stream of positive influences and impressions to help him formulate and reinforce his sense of himself. Reading books about other black boys and men, whether real or fictional, is one way for him to absorb the values of self-awareness, self-esteem, and confidence and to counterbalance the other messages he gets about being an African American.

And finally, we say to you: Read these books for yourself. We are always looking for ways to connect with our children, to find common ground for safe, nonthreatening conversations. We have found that discussing a book is often an excellent way to learn what your child is thinking and to open lines of communication.

Abraham's Battle: A Novel of Gettysburg [261]

Written by Sara Harrell Banks

Hardcover: Atheneum
Published 1999

Abraham, an aging freed slave who lives and works in Gettysburg, Pennsylvania, in 1863, realizes that he must contribute to the Civil War effort that will ultimately abolish slavery. He becomes an ambulance driver for the Union Army, transporting the wounded from the historic Battle of Gettysburg. On one sojourn onto the battlefield, Abraham finds a mortally wounded Confederate soldier, Lamar, whom he had occasion to meet, man-to-man, days before when the young man was on a scouting mission. Here, lying on the battlefield, Lamar is neither black nor white, friend nor foe, but a human being who needs help. This book of historical fiction details the key events that led to the battle that helped determine the final outcome of the Civil War. **Nonstandard English.**

> "*And while he didn't think anybody was much concerned about a solitary colored man bearing a wounded rebel. . . . he was scared to take the chance. . . . 'We gone' take this boy back to our side. They'll take care of him.'*"

Across the Lines [262]

Written by Carolyn Reeder

Hardcover: Atheneum
Softcover: Avon Camelot, Avon
Published 1997

Edward, a young slave master, and Simon, his young slave and playmate, are separated when their plantation home is overtaken by Union soldiers. Edward flees with his family to a Southern city, to a much different life than he had ever before experienced. Simon, at first happy to be liberated, is now on his own, working from hand to mouth to earn his keep, hoping that he will find somewhere to call home and someone to call friend. The lives of the two boys are still in deep contrast, as they live on different sides of the Civil War battle line. This eventful and captivating book is for more advanced young readers.

Adventures of Midnight Son [263]

Written by Denise Lewis Patrick ☆ 120

Hardcover: Henry Holt
Published 1997

Midnight Son was a thirteen-year-old slave who escaped to Mexico where he found freedom and the adventures of a lifetime as a ranch hand. Midnight's early family life and daring escape are described in compelling detail in the first half of the book. In the second half, Midnight grows to manhood and is challenged to become one of the best cowboys in the region. He undertakes his new position on the ranch with vigor and encounters several dangerous but exciting challenges, such as driving his cattle herd through a twister. Underscoring the story is Midnight's struggle with his feelings about leaving his family behind in slavery, as he builds a new life among people who respect his humanity. *The Longest Ride* [309] is the sequel to this book.

Ajeemah and His Son [264]

Written by James Berry

Softcover: HarperTrophy, HarperCollins
Published 1991

Ajeemah and his son, Atu, are ambushed and kidnapped by slave traders as they walk near their African village. Brought to Jamaica, they are sold to different plantations. Anguished by their loss of homeland, family, and each other, the two reluctantly obey their masters, even as they secretly plan their escapes. Though neither knows the whereabouts of the other they are somehow connected, feeling each other's pain—to the extent that Ajeemah is stricken with grief at the exact moment of his son's death. Ajeemah never does escape, but he is freed in 1838 when slavery in Jamaica comes to an end.

Anthony Burns: The Defeat and Triumph of a Fugitive Slave [265]

Written by Virginia Hamilton

Hardcover: Alfred A. Knopf
Softcover: Random House
Published 1988

Anthony Burns was an escaped slave who was recaptured in Massachusetts shortly before the Civil War. With strong support of Northern abolitionists, he stood trial to try to win his freedom, but was returned to his master in Virginia under the Fugitive Slave Act. His freedom was later purchased by his Northern supporters and he was given a scholarship to Oberlin College, where he studied for the ministry. The early death of this historical figure at the age of twenty-eight was, no doubt, a result of the stresses and hardships endured in his young life.

Anthony's Big Surprise [266]

Written by Wade Hudson

Softcover: Just Us
Published 1998

Anthony is a member of NEATE, a wholesome group of kids named for the first letter in each member's name: Naimah, Elizabeth, Anthony, Tayesha, and Eddie. In the main story, Anthony comes face to face with his father, whom he has never met and whom he believed to be dead. Reeling from the reality, Anthony questions his single mother's explanation of past events and learns the truth. Other titles in the NEATE series are *NEATE to the Rescue* and *Elizabeth's Wish*.

Cassandra Burns McDonald likes to read to Connor, age 4, at bedtime, especially bedtime favorites like *The Snowy Day* and *Joshua's Night Whispers*.

At the Plate with Ken Griffey, Jr. [267]

Written by Matt Christopher

Softcover: Little, Brown
Published 1997

Ken Griffey Jr. learned the game of baseball at the feet of his famous father, Ken Griffey Sr. The number one sports writer for kids, Matt Christopher, shares Griffey Jr.'s quest to join the game that both he and his father love. The story covers Griffey's early days hanging out at Yankee Stadium with his father, through his own stardom as a long-standing member of the Seattle Mariners. A center insert contains ten black-and-white photographs of the young baseball star, his major league statistics, and a timeline of his career highlights. Another book in the series is *At the Plate with Mo Vaughn*.

Basketball Legends Series [268]

Written by various authors

Hardcover: Chelsea House
Published 1991–1995

Some of the most dynamic names in basketball are featured in this biographical series. Written for young sports enthusiasts, each book profiles the personal lives and careers of the athlete and includes details of important career milestones, interesting photographs, and career statistics. The Basketball Legends series includes books about Kareem Abdul-Jabbar, Charles Barkley, Kobe Bryant, Wilt Chamberlain, Julius Erving, Patrick Ewing, Anfernee Hardaway, Grant Hill, Juwan Howard, Magic Johnson, Michael Jordan, Reggie Miller, Alonzo Mourning, Hakeem Olajuwon, Shaquille O'Neal, Scottie Pippin, David Robinson, and Dennis Rodman.

Black Diamond: The Story of the Negro Baseball Leagues [269]

Written by Patricia C. McKissack ☆ 96 and Fredrick McKissack Jr.

Hardcover and softcover: Scholastic
Published 1994

The extraordinary history of the black baseball players who were a part of the Negro Baseball Leagues is told in this well-documented book. The players persevered through racism, the Great Depression, and personal indignities in order to play the game that they loved. The comprehensive story is peppered with short anecdotes about individual players such as Satchel Paige, Josh Gibson, and Buck Leonard. Photographs of teams, players, historical documents, and newspaper headlines add a special dimension to the story.

Black Hands, White Sails: The Story of African-American Whalers [270]

Written by Patricia C. McKissack ☆ 96
and Fredrick L. McKissack

Coretta Scott King Honor: Author

Hardcover: Scholastic
Published 1999

Another little-known story from the chapters of African American history is told in this intriguing book about blacks in the whaling industry, 1730–1880. Blacks, many of whom were fleeing slavery, signed on to work on whaling vessels for the better life it offered. African American whalers not only contributed to the whaling industry but also played critical roles in the Underground Railroad. A number of authentic black-and-white photographs, drawings, and documents help punctuate the story.

Black Hoops: The History of African Americans in Basketball [271]

Written by Fredrick McKissack, Jr.

Hardcover: Scholastic
Published 1999

This is a well-researched history of African Americans in basketball from the inception of the game to the present, when blacks dominate the popular sport. Included are many black-and-white photographs and stories about many of the greatest black players, such as Dr. J., Magic Johnson, Michael Jordan, and Shaquille O'Neal, and teams like the Harlem Rens and the Chicago Globetrotters (yes, Chicago). Young readers will learn about how the Civil Rights movement spilled over into basketball, forcing the integration of the game. There is even a chapter on black women in basketball, offering a complete view of the sport.

Synthia
Saint James

AUTHOR AND
ILLUSTRATOR

"I have no recollections of any picture books featuring black children in the 1950s. But, in retrospect, I know for a fact that my generation would have grown up with heightened self-esteem if we had experienced seeing our true selves in books. I wish that as a child, I had had the many historical books on black achievers in all fields available to me."

OUR FAVORITES FROM
SYNTHIA SAINT JAMES

Snow on Snow on Snow [75]

Tukama Tootles the Flute: A Tale from the Antilles [79]

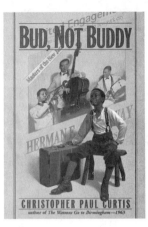

Bud, Not Buddy [272]

Written by Christopher Paul Curtis

Hardcover: Delacorte
Published 1999

Coretta Scott King Award: Author
Newbery Award

In the Depression era, a motherless ten-year-old boy named Bud is determined to find his father. The only clue he has, a flyer about Herman E. Calloway, bandleader of the Dusky Devastators of the Depression, is enough to start Bud on an unforgettable journey. Bud travels by hopping trains and survives by his wits, developed far beyond his years, in this fast-paced story.

Captain Africa: The Battle for Egyptia [273]

Written and illustrated by Dwayne J. Ferguson

Softcover: Africa World
Published 1992

Captain Africa, a black superhero, does battle with Terror Supreme, his evil nemesis in this high-tech futuristic story. Captain Africa must save humanity from Terror Supreme's diabolical plot to destroy the world with a devastating superweapon. Fast-paced and exciting, this story offers young readers the thrill of the adventure and, for the first time, both the superhero and the bad guy are black!

The Captive [274]

Written by Joyce Hansen

Hardcover and softcover: Scholastic
Published 1994

"*I** was seized by a sudden jolt of terror. . . . I had been taken across the seas far away from all I knew and loved, to the land of the white foreigners who would try to make me a slave. I was kidnapped— a captive.*"

Kofi, a West African prince, is betrayed by a fellow countryman and stolen away from his family, friends, and Sierra Leone homeland by slave traders in 1788. Young readers will travel with him from the time of his terrifying bondage and voyage over the Atlantic in a slave ship to his landing in America, where he is sold into slavery. As Kofi struggles to survive in his treacherous new land, his West African family copes with the loss of their son. This riveting novel, told in wrenching detail from Kofi's perspective, will intrigue young readers, sensitizing them to the unfathomable tragedy of the victims—both the enslaved young man and the family left behind.

Chevrolet Saturdays [275]

Written by Candy Dawson Boyd

Hardcover: Simon & Schuster
Softcover: Puffin, Penguin USA
Published 1993

Joey Davis, a fourth-grade boy, faces a very difficult year of adjustment at home and at school in this realistic novel. Joey resents his mother's remarriage and his stepfather's persistent attempts to bond with him. Joey is also troubled by a difficult relationship with a teacher who tries to move him into a special education program, even though he has demonstrated an amazing aptitude for science. Joey's character is well developed as he struggles with his problems and receives unexpected support from his stepfather.

Come All You Brave Soldiers: Blacks in the Revolutionary War [276]

Written by Clinton Cox

Hardcover: Scholastic
Published 1999

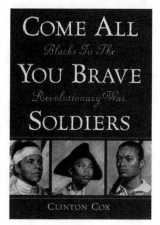

Over five thousand black soldiers fought for America's independence during the Revolutionary War. The stories of these courageous but largely unsung patriots are told in this well-researched book. Accounts of such men as Peter Salem and Cuff Whitmore, who were there when the first shots were fired at Lexington and Concord; or Lemuel Haynes and Barzillai Lew, who fought with Ethan Allen and his Green Mountain Boys, will make young readers proud of the role that blacks played in the making of America.

Darnell Rock Reporting [277]

Written by Walter Dean Myers ☆ 112

Hardcover and softcover: Delacorte, Bantam Doubleday Dell
Published 1994

In this uplifting story, Miss Seldes, the school librarian, understands that Darnell needs a constructive connection to the school to keep him out of trouble. She suggests that he become involved in writing for the school newspaper, an idea that he hates. He decides to approach his newspaper assignment with as little effort as possible. So no one is more surprised than he when he becomes involved in an intriguing story that captures everyone's attention and casts him in an important role as the reporter. Darnell's sense of self is immediately elevated as he begins to recognize his strengths and the possibilities for his life.

Denzel Washington: Actor [278]

Written by Anne Hill

Hardcover and softcover: Chelsea House
Published 1990

Denzel Washington is one of dozens of noteworthy African American men from past and present who are profiled in the Black Americans of Achievement series. In this book, the story of the accomplished actor is compellingly told. The book tracks Washington's life from his early days as the son of a struggling but strong single mother through his rise to acclaim as a movie star. The series includes the stories of other black male achievers, including Alex Haley, Thurgood Marshall, Josh Gibson, Romare Bearden, and fifty-six others.

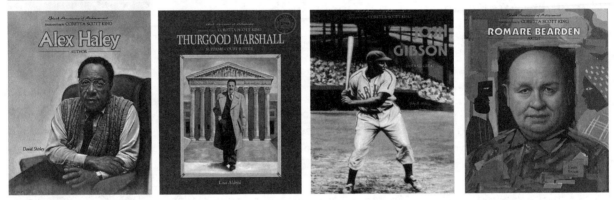

Donovan's Word Jar [279]

Written by Monalisa DeGross
Illustrated by Cheryl Hanna

Hardcover and softcover: HarperCollins
Published 1994

Some kids collect trading cards, buttons, or bottle caps, but Donovan collects words. Whenever he sees a new or interesting word, he writes it on a slip of paper and puts it in his word jar. When his jar becomes too full, he must find a solution to that problem. This popular chapter book may motivate children to consider building their own vocabularies. There is also a wonderful underlying story line about a positive relationship between Donovan and his family.

Drew and the Bub Daddy Showdown [280]

Written and illustrated by Robb Armstrong

Softcover: Trophy Chapter, HarperCollins
Published 1996

Uncannily, when the cast is removed from eight-year-old Drew's arm, he can suddenly draw expertly, and he creates and draws a comic book series about Super Agent Mason Stone. Drew's enterprising friends sell copies of the comics, elevating Drew to instant celebrity status at school. Drew and his friends use their new-found income to buy Bub Daddy, a two-foot-long striped bubble gum. Drew's new endeavor draws fire from a tough teacher, the school bullies, and his parents. In an interesting effect, Drew's comic strip is embedded in the story, making it a two-for-one hit! Another adventure about Drew and his friends can be found in *Drew and the Homeboy Question* [281].

Drew and the Homeboy Question [281]

Written and illustrated by Robb Armstrong

Softcover: HarperTrophy, HarperCollins
Published 1997

Drew and his homeboys are graduating from the sixth grade and bound for Drummond Junior High in the fall. But after a school-yard shooting and several other incidents, Drew's parents decide that Drummond isn't the right school for him. When they begin to explore private schools, especially an all-white preppie school in the suburbs, Drew's friends turn on him. Drew's life turns upside down as he passes through a potentially life-changing crossroad in his young life. Another book in this series is *Drew and the Bub Daddy Showdown* [280].

Drylongso [282]

Written by Virginia Hamilton
Illustrated by Jerry Pinkney

Hardcover: Harcourt Brace Jovanovich
Published 1992

A great wall of dust sweeps across the land during the drought, blowing a tall "stick-fella" into the home of young Lindy and her family. The "stick fella," named Drylongso, brings seeds and hope to the struggling family who are desperate for rain for their crops. More importantly, Drylongso brings a dowser rod and helps the family find a deeply buried spring. The story is warm, the characters are compassionate, and the illustrations are expressive in this mature picture story.

Escape to Freedom: A Play about Young Frederick Douglass [283]

Written by Ossie Davis   **Coretta Scott King Award: Author**

Softcover: Puffin, Penguin
Published 1978

> "*Keep us ignorant, and we would always be his slaves!...Come hell or high water—even if it cost me my life—I was determined to read.*"

The early life of Frederick Douglass is presented in this play, which is written for a cast of seven young actors. Readers can enjoy the script for their own pleasure and enrichment or perform it with friends. In either case, they will learn about Frederick's consuming quest to learn to read and the risks that he took to do so. His literacy led Frederick to a plan for his own escape and helped pave the way for his destiny as a powerful African American leader.

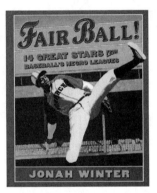

Fair Ball!: 14 Great Stars from Baseball's Negro Leagues [284]

Written and illustrated by Jonah Winter

Hardcover: Scholastic
Published 1999

Fourteen unsung heroes of the game of baseball are at last recognized in this book about the little-known but talented members of the Negro Baseball Leagues. The players, such as Rube Foster and Bingo DeMoss, are presented in an oversized baseball-card format, with a colorful illustration of the athlete on one side of the page and vital statistics and a career profile on the other. Fans of the game will enjoy this book of almost-lost baseball greats.

Finding Buck McHenry [285]

Written by Alfred Slote

Softcover: HarperTrophy, HarperCollins
Published 1991

Eleven-year-old Jason is bumped from his Little League team to another—supposedly an expansion team. But in his heart he believes it is because his game skills are not as good as those of some of the other players. When Mr. Henry, the school custodian, takes an interest in Jason and the "not quite yet" team and becomes their coach, the small group rallies around him. But then they make the mistake of thinking that Mr. Henry is actually Buck McHenry, a retired star player from the old Negro Leagues. Jason and his friends find that they were wrong about their coach's identity but absolutely right about what he brings to their team.

First in the Field: Baseball Hero Jackie Robinson [286]

Written by Derek T. Dingle

Hardcover: Hyperion
Published 1998

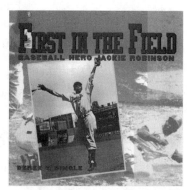

This photo-filled biography of the acclaimed Jackie Robinson offers a thorough portrait of the man who broke the color barrier in major league baseball. The comprehensive story includes details about Jackie's family life, education, military life, and baseball career, both in the Negro Leagues and in the Major Leagues. A three-page addendum at the end of the book details other important milestones in black sports history from the beginning of record-keeping in 1845, when the New York Knickerbockers allowed blacks and integrated teams to play, to 1997, when Tiger Woods became the first African American to win the Master's Golf Tournament.

Forty Acres and Maybe a Mule [287]

Written by Harriette Gillem Robinet ☆ 128

Hardcover: Jean Karl, Atheneum
Published 1998

Twelve-year-old Pascal, his brother, and other newly emancipated slaves band together as a family in search of General Sherman's promise that there would be forty acres and maybe a mule for every ex-slave family in 1865, at the end of the Civil War. This credible work of historical fiction delivers an emotional story of the family's struggle to succeed on their small farm against all odds. In spite of their legal right to be free, the young family faces the treachery and violence of the white Southerners who stop at nothing to oppress them.

Frederick Douglass: The Last Days of Slavery [288]

Written by William Miller
Illustrated by: Cedric Lucas ☆ 88

Hardcover and softcover: Lee & Low
Published 1995

Frederick Douglass was born a slave in 1817. Douglass, however, was always independent, unafraid to challenge others or to ask questions. An overseer targets Douglass, intent on breaking his spirit and free-thinking attitude. Douglass fights back, earning the respect of the overseer and demonstrating the pride and dignity for which he later becomes known. It is easy for young readers to appreciate this fictionalized biography.

Free to Dream: The Making of a Poet, Langston Hughes [289]

Written by Audrey Osofsky

Hardcover: Lothrop, Lee & Shepard
Published 1996

The story of the life and times of Langston Hughes, one of the most renowned African American poets of the twentieth century, is told in rich detail in this biography. The well-researched text, accompanied by many black-and-white photographs, chronicles the diverse experiences that served as inspiration for this profound poet. A number of his poems, including the famous "Hold Fast to Dreams," are presented, demonstrating his poetic genius.

The Friendship [290]

Written by Mildred D. Taylor
Illustrated by Max Ginsburg

Hardcover: Dial
Softcover: Puffin
Published 1987

In rural Mississippi in 1933, the lines between blacks and whites were clearly drawn. That is why Cassie and her brothers were so nervous when Old Tom Bee, an elderly black man, defiantly called white storekeeper John Wallace by his first name. Old Tom Bee's dignity and John Wallace's honor are explored in this tense, dramatic story. ***Nonstandard English. Use of N Word.***

From Slave to Civil War Hero: The Life and Times of Robert Smalls [291]

Written by Michael L. Cooper

Hardcover: Lodestar, Penguin USA
Published 1994

Robert Smalls courageously escaped slavery to join the Union Army in 1862. Smalls served as a Union soldier and distinguished himself as an advocate for newly free slaves and as an elected U.S. congressman. This interesting biography is supplemented with many black-and-white photographs, maps, and illustrations of Civil War scenes. The description of the war, the social and political climate, and other relevant details of the era help to establish a rich view of the time and of Smalls's role in history.

Ghost Train [292]

Written by Jess Mowry

Hardcover: Henry Holt
Published 1996

Thirteen-year-old Remi and his neighbor, Niya, are drawn into a murder mystery in this ghostly tale set in a tough Oakland, California, neighborhood. Remi, a recent Haitian immigrant, and the street-wise Niya witness a frightening murder and coverup in a shipyard at an Oakland dock. The only problem is that the event happened fifty years before. Inexplicably, they become a part of the scene and confront the murderer in an attempt to lay the haunted case to rest forever. This suspense-filled, fast-paced story will draw young readers in, and hold them, until the surprise ending. *Use of N word.*

Go Fish [293]

Written by Mary Stolz
Illustrated by Pat Cummings

Hardcover and softcover: HarperCollins
Published 1991

Thomas spends a day with his grandfather, who amazes him with interesting bits and pieces of information about everything from fossils and dinosaurs to ancestral stories and folktales. In this warm story of male bonding, there is even time for a trip to the fishing pier and a game of Go Fish. Other books about Thomas and his grandfather are *Stealing Home* [336], *Storm in the Night* [231], and *Coco Grimes*.

Gold Diggers [294]

Written by Kwasi Koranteng
Illustrated by Pauline King

Softcover: Chelsea House
Published 1992

Kanjaga puts himself in peril when he accepts a job as an undercover agent. In this suspenseful short novel, Kanjaga is assigned to infiltrate and break up a ring of gold diggers who are stealing gold from the national mines of his small African country. Kanjaga enters the underworld disguised as an escaped convict in order to gain the acceptance of the criminals. Four of his police colleagues have died on this assignment, so he must use his wits and cunning, and be extremely careful not to expose himself.

Got Game? [295]

Written by Robb Armstrong
Illustrated by Bruce Smith

Softcover: HarperActive, HarperCollins
Published 1998

One of Patrick's best friends, Keith, is being disrespected by another friend and teammate, Zo. Ever since Zo's birthday he lords his age advantage and basketball skills over the younger Keith. Zo insists that Keith be the waterboy for the Bulldogs, their basketball team, rather than play, and he won't even give Keith the chance to show what he can do. Keith seizes his moment, however, and shows Zo and the rest of the team that he is worthy of their respect on the court. This book is one in the series based on the fictionalized young life of Patrick Ewing and other NBA greats. Other titles in the Patrick's Pals series include: *In Your Face* [299], *Large and In Charge!*, *Runnin' with the Big Dawgs* [328], *Schoolin', Stuffin' It* [337], and *Trashmaster* [344].

Have A Happy . . .: A Novel about Kwanzaa [296]

Written by Mildred Pitts Walter ☆ 174
Illustrated by Carole Byard

Hardcover: Lothrop, Lee & Shepard, William Morrow
Softcover: Camelot Avon, Hearst
Published 1989

Ten-year-old Chris and his family usually celebrate Christmas, but he always feels a little let down because his birthday falls during the same time and gets lost in the hustle and bustle of the season. The family enjoys a different kind of holiday, however, when Chris's uncle introduces them to the African American celebration of Kwanzaa. Chris and his family experience a more meaningful season as they focus on each other and on their proud heritage.

The Hundred Penny Box [297]

Written by Sharon Bell Mathis   **Newbery Honor Book**
Illustrated by Leo and Diane Dillon

Hardcover and softcover: Penguin USA
Published 1975

Michael's great-great-aunt Dew, who is one hundred years old, lives with him and his family. Although her mind is not always sharp, she is clear about the importance of her box full of pennies—one minted in every year of her life. Michael is defiantly protective of his aunt and her old battered box against his mother, who wants to replace it with a smaller, neater box. This is an intimate story about sensitivity, compassion, love, and respect in a family.

Joseph Mayfield reads to Matthew, age 3, mostly on the weekends. "Some of my favorite books to read have wonderful pictures of boys going about their everyday experiences, like *Jamal's Busy Day* and *Jonathan and His Mommy*."

If You Please, President Lincoln [298]

Written by Harriette Gillem Robinet ☆ 128

Hardcover: Atheneum, Simon & Schuster
Published 1995

In the midst of the Civil War, President Lincoln considered proposals to establish colonies of liberated slaves on offshore islands. In this fictional story, a young runaway slave becomes part of a poorly conceived and unauthorized plan to create such a colony on a small island. Four hundred ex-slaves are recaptured by an unscrupulous captain and transported to an island off Haiti, where there are no provisions for their survival. When the few remaining victims are returned to America, they are falsely rumored to have lived like savages—cannibalizing, raping, and murdering one another for survival. This fascinating but emotionally tugging novel will evoke anger at the injustice and racism that the group experienced, but pride in their responsibility and resourcefulness.

In Your Face [299]

Written by Robb Armstrong
Illustrated by Bruce Smith

Softcover: HarperActive, HarperCollins
Published 1998

Patrick Ewing and his basketball teammates, known as the Bulldogs, are challenged to a game of hoops by the Warriors, the meanest, toughest team in town. The game gets out of hand when tempers flare and the play gets more and more physical. When things are about to turn very ugly, the coach steps in to break up the game. Soon a fight challenge is issued by Carlos, captain of the Warriors. The Bulldogs depend on Patrick to stand up for their reputation and team pride. Face to face with Carlos, Patrick realizes that violence will only lead to more of the same. He makes the tough decision to end the nonsense by turning and walking away. This book features Patrick Ewing and fellow NBA players Dikembe Mutombo and Alonzo Mourning as adolescents in the fictionalized Patrick's Pals series. Other titles include: *Got Game?* [295], *Large and In Charge!, Runnin' with the Big Dawgs* [328], *Schoolin', Stuffin' It* [337], and *Trashmaster* [344].

The Journal of Joshua Loper: A Black Cowboy, The Chisholm Trail, 1871 [300]

Written by Walter Dean Myers ☆ 112

Hardcover: Scholastic
Published 1999

Sixteen-year-old Joshua Loper enters manhood the day he joins a cattle drive heading up the Chisholm Trail from Texas to Kansas. Joshua records his experiences in his daily journal from May through August, the duration of the drive. His reflections include personal accounts of the difficult journey, including dramatic stories about his challenging on-the-job training, stampeding cattle, and Indian encounters. Joshua's very personal diary, found after the real-life cowboy's death, in 1920, is a significant first-hand account of life as a black cowboy.

Junebug [301]

Written by Alice Mead

Hardcover: Farrar, Straus and Giroux
Softcover: Yearling, Bantam Doubleday Dell
Published 1995

Things could not be worse for nine-year-old Junebug. His best friend Darnell just ran away to avoid a confrontation with a drug lord. His Aunt Jolita is mixed up with the wrong crowd and fighting with his mother. And the reading teacher who was helping his little sister has just quit out of fear of his rough New Haven, Connecticut, neighborhood. What's more, Junebug is about to turn ten years old, an age that he fears because that is when drugs, guns, and crime influences come into young boys' lives. Junebug is distracted from all of his problems by his dream of becoming a sailor. He writes his dreams on notes and stuffs them inside glass bottles that he launches into the sea. Junebug's story is one of hope and the possibilities for inner-city children to rise above their challenging environments. A sequel is *Junebug and the Reverend* [302].

Irene Smalls

AUTHOR

"I first became a writer in kindergarten when my teacher, Miss Loretta Abbott, read to us the poetry of Paul Lawrence Dunbar and James Weldon Johnson. Our standard reading text was *Fun with Dick and Jane,* but Miss Abbott read to us about the 'Lil' brown baby with the sparklin' eyes.' I fell in love with language and reading for I knew I was that lil' brown baby girl."

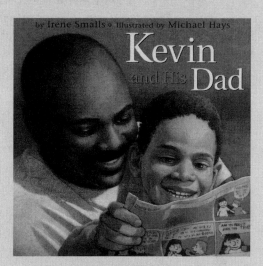

OUR FAVORITES FROM
IRENE SMALLS

Because You're Lucky [93]

Jonathan and His Mommy [50]

Kevin and His Dad [164]

A Strawbeater's Thanksgiving [233]

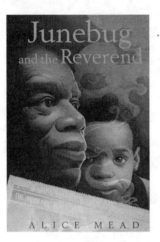

Junebug and the Reverend [302]

Written by Alice Mead

Hardcover: Farrar, Straus and Giroux
Published 1998

Ten-year-old Junebug makes an honest attempt to adjust when the family moves to a new neighborhood because his mother has taken a job supervising a group home for the elderly. Junebug is challenged by a number of adolescent travails, like fitting in at the new school at the end of the school year, a confrontation with a bully, and hardest of all, accepting his mother's new boyfriend. The confused boy gets unexpected support and understanding from an unlikely friend, Reverend Ashford. The reverend, one of the home's elderly residents, gets as much as he gives from this touching relationship. The story is the sequel to *Junebug* [301].

Just Like Martin [303]

Written by Ossie Davis

Hardcover: Silver Burdett
Softcover: Puffin
Published 1992

Young Stone is a member of his church's youth group and a devoted follower of the nonviolent philosophies of Dr. Martin Luther King Jr. When a racist's bomb explodes in his Sunday school classroom, killing two of his friends, Stone demonstrates his commitment by organizing his peers for a controversial nonviolent children's march. Stone must defy his father, who is much more militant, in this moving story set in the racially charged 1960s.

Justin and the Best Biscuits in the World [304]

Written by Mildred Pitts Walter ☆ 174   Coretta Scott King Award: Author

Illustrated by Catherine Stock

Hardcover: Lothrop, Lee & Shepard
Softcover: Bullseye, Random House
Published 1986

Young Justin lives in a female-run house where he is overwhelmed by the chores that are heaped on him by his mother and sisters. So he is excited when his grandfather invites him to his ranch out West. During the visit, Justin learns how to do men's work, but also learns that doing dishes, folding clothes, and making beds are not just for women. Furthermore, Grandpa teaches him to bake biscuits—the best in the world. The biscuits are entered in a baking contest and win first prize. The only thing missing from this entertaining story is the recipe for those biscuits!

Kid Caramel, Private Investigator: Case of the Missing Ankh [305]

Written by Dwayne Ferguson
Illustrated by Don Tate

Softcover: Just Us
Published 1996

Kid Caramel, fifth-grade sleuth, and his friend Earnie solve the mystery of a stolen crystal ankh that was taken from the city museum exhibit. Keen powers of observation, logic, and a creative plan to catch the thief help the two crack the case in this fun, fast-moving book. Young readers will enjoy solving the mystery with Kid and Earnie. A second book, *Kid Caramel, Private Investigator: The Werewolf of PS 40* [306] is also available.

Kid Caramel, Private Investigator: The Werewolf of PS 40 [306]

Written by Dwayne J. Ferguson
Illustrated by Don Tate

Softcover: Just Us
Published 1998

Kid Caramel and his best friend Earnie are on their second intriguing case. When all of the neighborhood pets begin to disappear, Kid Caramel begins to ask some questions. But the answers suggest only one thing—that a werewolf is involved. Since Kid Caramel knows that there is no such thing as a werewolf, he begins to put two and two together until he uncovers the real culprit. Young readers will enjoy analyzing the clues to see if they can solve the mystery before Kid Caramel does. These young sleuths were introduced in *Kid Caramel, Private Investigator: Case of the Missing Ankh* [305].

The Kidnapped Prince: The Life of Olaudah Equiano [307]

Written by Olaudah Equiano
Adapted by Ann Cameron

Softcover: Alfred A. Knopf
Published 1995

Eleven-year-old Olaudah Equiano was kidnapped by African slavers from his Benin homeland in 1755. He learned to read and write during his captivity and documented his experiences as a slave in his autobiography. Olaudah describes his life with his family in Africa prior to his abduction, and many of his brutal experiences such as the Middle Passage to the Americas. This book, adapted from Olaudah's personal writings, is a profound view from one who lived the dark reality.

Leon's Story [308]

Written by Leon Walter Tillage
Illustrated by Susan L. Roth

Hardcover: Farrar, Straus, and Giroux
Published 1997

> *"I remember that as a young boy I used to look in the mirror and I would curse my color, my blackness."*

True stories from the author's memories of his childhood as a sharecropper's son in rural North Carolina are told in this riveting book. The stories—many painful recollections of oppression, humiliation, and racism—lay the groundwork for Leon's involvement in the civil rights movement many years later. Leon's regular refrain, by way of explanation for things that had no acceptable explanation, is "That's just the way it was." Leon tells his story in a very conversational style that will help young readers understand what it really meant to be a black American just thirty short years ago.

The Longest Ride [309]

Written by Denise Lewis Patrick ☆ 120

Hardcover: Henry Holt
Published 1999

Fifteen-year-old Midnight Son sets out on a quest from Colorado to Louisiana to find his family at the end of the Civil War. Midnight passes through an Indian village during his journey and is compelled to help two new friends, brother and sister Eagle Eye and Winter Mary, whose people are under attack by the United States Calvary. Midnight is brave and responsible beyond his years in this dramatic, action-packed story, the sequel to *Adventures of Midnight Son* [263].

> "*Midnight had heard so many stories from other cowboys at the Crazy Eight and in the towns they'd passed through about the 'bloodthirsty Injuns' and 'murdering red men.' Yet the one Indian he'd really known was a hardworking man like any other.*"

Male Writers [310]

Edited by Richard Rennert

Hardcover: Chelsea House
Published 1994

Young readers will be inspired by the stories of eight of the most noteworthy African American male writers, from contemporary authors like Alex Haley and James Baldwin to historical writers like Richard Wright and Langston Hughes. Each writer's story is told in a brief essay that includes details about his background and writing legacy. A black-and-white portrait of each author gives faces to the talented pioneers.

Martin Luther King [311]

Written by Rosemary L. Bray
Illustrated by Malcah Zeldis

Hardcover and softcover: William Morrow
Published 1995

The life and works of Martin Luther King Jr. are captured in forty-seven over-sized pages of text and bright folk art in this exceptional book. The text begins by covering Martin's early life, when his childhood experiences began to shape his sensibilities. The major events of Martin's life are touched upon, including the day he became aware of and embraced Gandhi's philosophy of nonviolent protest, and his marriage to Coretta Scott. Every significant civil rights event during Martin's adult life is detailed, framing a young reader's understanding of the era and of King's leadership role.

Me, Mop, and the Moondance Kid [312]

Written by Walter Dean Myers ☆ 112
Illustrated by Rodney Pate

Softcover: Yearling, Bantam Doubleday Dell
Published 1988

T. J. and Moondance are brothers who have been recently adopted from the Dominican Academy, an orphanage. Their best friend, Mop, is still without a family, and the orphanage is about to close. The three kids play on a baseball team together, so they plan for Mop to attract the coach's attention and to entice him and his wife to adopt her. T. J., on the other hand, is reluctant to participate because he does not want his new adoptive father to see how poorly he plays. The story unfolds through T. J.'s engaging first-person style. Several black-and-white illustrations add a fun touch to the short novel. The sequel to this book is *Mop, Moondance, and the Nagasaki Knights*.

The Middle of Somewhere: A Story of South Africa [313]

Written by Sheila Gordon

Hardcover: Richard Jackson, Orchard
Softcover: Bantam Doubleday Dell
Published 1990

Young Rebecca, who lives in a black township in South Africa, is afraid of being forced out of her home. The government wants to relocate her family and neighbors to a less developed area in order to accommodate expansion for white suburbanites. The villagers protest the attempts to move them, and Rebecca's father is arrested after a community-wide demonstration. The evils of apartheid come through strongly in this novel of a family's determination to stay together in their village.

Mississippi Chariot [314]

Written by Harriette Gillem Robinet ☆ 128

Hardcover: Atheneum, Macmillan
Softcover: Aladdin, Simon & Schuster
Published 1994

In 1936, the lives of a sharecropper's family are forever changed when twelve-year-old Shortening Bread Jackson takes control of the family's problems. In this dramatic and suspenseful novel, Shortening Bread devises a plan to force the release of his father, who is serving time, unjustly, on a Mississippi chain gang. Shortening Bread's ploy is dangerous not only to his family, but to the entire black community. The courageous boy saves his father and then his family from the wrath of their white oppressors with his own wit and strong sense of survival.

Mouse Rap [315]

Written by Walter Dean Myers ☆ 112

Softcover: HarperTrophy, HarperCollins
Published 1990

Every chapter of this spirited story begins with a rap from the self-confident fourteen-year-old, Mouse. Mouse believes that being cool is essential. His summer is full of adolescent challenges: His prodigal father returns after an eight-year absence and tries to become a part of his life again; then a new girl starts coming on to him while Sheri, a friend from his crew, tries to get him to compete in a dance contest. Most intriguing, though, is the rumor that a stash of money from 1930s mobsters is hidden in an abandoned building in his Harlem neighborhood, which Mouse and the crew plan to find. Young readers will be absorbed by this hip, contemporary story.

> "You can call me Mouse, 'cause that's my tag
> I'm into it all, everything's my bag
> You know I can run, you know I can hoop
> I can do it alone, or in a group."

No Turning Back: A Novel of South Africa [316]

Written by Beverly Naidoo

Hardcover: HarperCollins
Published 1997

An abusive stepfather forces twelve-year-old Sipho from his township home into the streets of Johannesburg. There, he joins a gang of other *malunde* (homeless) children living in the streets, learning to survive the harsh realities of street life. Scrambling for every morsel of food, every nook or cranny to sleep in, and security from angry white antagonists, Sipho is given brief refuge by a white merchant and his family. This powerful novel, written in post-apartheid South Africa just prior to Mandela's election, offers vital insight into contemporary life for some black children in that country.

Oh, Brother [317]

Written by Johniece Marshall Wilson

Softcover: Apple, Scholastic
Published 1988

Sibling relationships are tough enough, but they're even worse when two brothers, as different as night and day, share a room. In this entertaining story, Alex is the organized, industrious younger brother who is constantly victimized by his less disciplined, sloppy older brother, Andrew. Andrew frequently borrows Alex's bike and ultimately loses it, which makes it very difficult for Alex to work his paper route. Andrew's friends tease and try to intimidate young Alex. There is plenty of anger and frustration between the two, but they are family, and they come through for each other when it really counts.

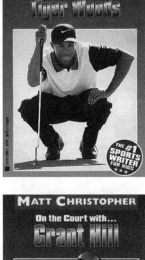

On the Course with Tiger Woods [318]

Written by Matt Christopher

Softcover: Little, Brown
Published 1998

Even at an early age, Tiger Woods is already a golfing legend. This book tells the story of Tiger's extraordinary talent, how it was developed and nurtured, and how he mastered every level of the game from junior amateur to professional. There are insights into Tiger's personality, which is marked by fierce determination and an unyielding competitiveness. A center insert includes ten black-and-white photographs, Tiger's amateur record and professional statistics, and a list of his professional credits and tournament earnings.

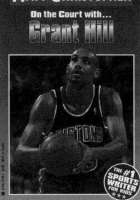

On the Court with Grant Hill [319]

Written by Matt Christopher

Softcover: Little, Brown
Published 1991

The astounding career of basketball great Grant Hill is told in this biographical profile. Hill's basketball prowess is traced from high school stardom through his rookie year on the NBA's Detroit Pistons. During his first year, Hill distinguished himself as an up-and-coming force in the game, winning the co-rookie of the year honor and a place on the All-Star Team. Ten black-and-white photographs, a statistical profile, and a list of Hill's career highlights are included. Other basketball players profiled in the On the Court series include Hakeem Olajuwon and Michael Jordan.

On the Field with Emmitt Smith [320]

Written by Matt Christopher

Softcover: Little, Brown
Published 1997

Emmitt Smith, one of the best running backs in professional football, is profiled in this book. Smith's career as a Dallas Cowboy is highlighted by a Rookie of the Year title, three Super Bowl wins, and four NFL rushing titles. The book covers each of Smith's football periods from his early college and rookie years through his Super Bowl face-off with the Pittsburgh Steelers in 1996. A center insert includes ten black-and-white photographs, a year-by-year list of statistics, and a time line of Smith's career highlights.

Pink and Say [321]

Written and illustrated by Patricia Polacco

Hardcover: Philomel
Published 1994

This heart-stinging true story has been passed down through the generations of the family of Sheldon Curtis (Say), a white Union soldier in the Civil War, and is offered in tribute to the black soldier, Pinkus Aylee (Pink), who befriended him. Pink found the wounded Say in a pasture and carried him to the home of his own mother for nursing and recovery. The two men, as Union soldiers, and the black woman, living alone in Confederate territory, defied the odds in this dramatic story. Their kindness cost Pink and his mother their lives but brought them Say's undying gratitude.

A Place in the Sun [322]

Written by Jill Rubalcaba

Hardcover: Clarion, Houghton Mifflin
Published 1997

Young Senmut accidentally kills a dove while carving the figure of Sekhmet, the goddess of healing, which he was making to help his critically ill father. He is sentenced to a life of hard labor at a life-draining mining camp for killing the sacred bird. Still, he is determined to try to save his father, so he steals a small amount of gold from the mines to gild the carving. He and the carving are discovered and delivered to the Pharaoh, whose son is near death. The power of the carving heals the stricken son and earns Senmut the honor of being named royal sculptor. This story, set in the thirteenth century B.C., provides an interesting view of ancient Egyptian culture and beliefs.

A Pony for Jeremiah [323]

Written by Robert H. Miller ☆ 104
Illustrated by Nneka Bennett

Hardcover and softcover: Silver Burdett, Simon & Schuster
Published 1996

Jeremiah and his family escape slavery and begin a new life in the Nebraska territory. Jeremiah asks his father for a new pony, so the two go on a great adventure and capture a wild one, to the envy of a young Cheyenne boy, who later becomes a friend. The horse refuses to be broken and will not stay in captivity, a feeling that Jeremiah can relate to, so he allows the wild animal to go free. One day, to Jeremiah's surprise, the pony returns, on its own terms, and becomes a willing part of his life.

Red Dog, Blue Fly: Football Poems [324]

Written by Sharon Bell Mathis
Illustrated by Jan Spivey Gilchrist

Softcover: Puffin, Penguin
Published 1991

Thirteen poems for young football lovers tell the story of the sport's season. Among the selections are "Touchdown," "Leg Broken," "Quarterback," and "Victory Banquet." If you have trouble getting your young jock to sit down and read (poetry or otherwise), perhaps this book will provide a breakthrough.

Reflections of a Black Cowboy: Pioneers [325]

Written by Robert H. Miller ☆ 104
Illustrated by Floyd Cooper

Hardcover: Silver Burdett
Published 1991

The stories of six African American pioneers are expressively told, adding them to the pages of American history. Young readers will read, perhaps for the first time, about York, an invaluable guide and interpreter on the Lewis and Clark Expedition; George Monroe, a unyielding Pony Express rider who delivered his mail, no matter what; Alvin Coffey, a black gold miner who bought his own freedom; and others. Each story is brought to life with great panache and a few well-placed black-and-white illustrations. The Reflections of a Black Cowboy series also includes titles on the Buffalo Soldiers, cowboys, and mountainmen.

The Righteous Revenge of Artemis Bonner [326]

Written by Walter Dean Myers ☆ 112

Softcover: HarperTrophy, HarperCollins
Published 1992

Artemis Bonner tells his side of the story in this spirited novel about a young man who travels to the Old West to hunt down the "murderous scalawag" Catfish Grimes, who killed his uncle. Artemis teams up with a young Cherokee boy named Frolic, and they chase the no-good Catfish and his girl-friend, Lucy Featherdip, across the West. Along the way, the two teams try to find the hidden treasure that Uncle Ugly buried before he died. Artemis and Frolic encounter the evil Catfish more than once, but they can't bring him to justice until the big gunfight scene at the end—and even then it is not over. The thoroughly entertaining story is humorously told by the proper young Artemis in a colorful language all his own.

> *"I heard that Catfish Grimes was not an easy sort to deal with, nor would the Featherdip woman be a pushover. But they would learn that Artemis Bonner knew more than what lay between the pages of his Hymnal and would not tolerate being taken lightly."*

Rimshots: Basketball Pix, Rolls, and Rhythms [327]

Written by Charles R. Smith, Jr.

Hardcover: Dutton, Penguin Putnam
Softcover: Puffin
Published 1999

Fourteen in-your-face selections about the game of basketball are guaranteed to get your young slam-dunker off the court and into a book, even if only for a few minutes. The selections—some poems, some stories, some personal reflections—are presented with bold graphic type and action photographs of the game.

> *"Wipe the sweat off the face with the left hand first. That's for Mom. Wipe the sweat off with the right hand. That's for Dad. Spin the ball in a quick vertical motion. Dribble, Dribble, Dribble, Deep breath. Eye on the rim. Shoot."*

Runnin' with the Big Dawgs [328]

Written by Robb Armstrong
Illustrated by Bruce Smith

Softcover: HarperActive, HarperCollins
Published 1998

Twelve-year-old Patrick Ewing is torn when Dawg, the captain of the hottest basketball team in the neighborhood, offers him a chance to play on his team. The problem is that being a Sky Walker means that he must play against his best friends on his former team, the Bulldogs, and even worse, that he can't even hang with his homies anymore. Patrick's overwhelming desire to be a Sky Walker clouds his judgment for a while, as he begins to do and say things against his Bulldog friends. In the end, Patrick must make the tough choice between his old friends and his new team. This book is in the Patrick's Pals series of fictionalized stories about Patrick Ewing and fellow NBA players Dikembe Mutombo and Alonzo Mourning as adolescents. Other books in the series include *Got Game?* [295], *In Your Face* [299], *Large and In Charge!*, *Schoolin', Stuffin' It* [337], and *Trashmaster* [344].

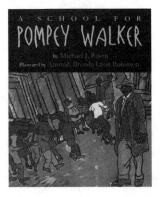

A School for Pompey Walker [329]

Written by Michael Rosen
Illustrated by Aminah Brenda Lynn Robinson

Hardcover: Harcourt Brace
Published 1995

A ninety-year-old man, Pompey, captivates a group of schoolchildren by discussing his experiences as a tortured slave many decades before. He shares a riveting story about his early days as an abused stable boy who yearned to go to school. One day his master's son-in-law, Jeremiah, who hated slavery, buys Pompey and immediately offers him his freedom. Pompey convinces Jeremiah to help him reach the North, where his freedom will be assured. Along the way, the two create a plan to make money for the journey. Over and over again, Jeremiah sells Pompey back into slavery and then helps him escape again. They share the money made with the dangerous con and put it to good use later, when Pompey fulfills his dream of establishing a school for black children.

Silent Thunder: A Civil War Story [330]

Written by Andrea Davis Pinkney
Illustrated by Jerry Pinkney

Hardcover: Hyperion Books for Children
Published 1999

Thirteen-year-old Rosco, a young slave on the Parnell plantation, hears the call of freedom—his "silent thunder." Having secretly learned to read by eavesdropping on the lessons of his young master, he is able to read newspapers about the Civil War and the impending Emancipation Proclamation. Rosco is torn between running away to join the Union Army to help fight for his own freedom and waiting for President Lincoln's proclamation. But how long must he wait? And how can he leave his mother and little sister behind in the hands of their cruel slave master? Rosco's dilemma, told in chapters alternating between his story and his sister's, comes to an exciting conclusion in this suspenseful book of historical fiction.

Sink or Swim: African-American Lifesavers of the Outer Banks [331]

Written by Carole Boston Weatherford

Hardcover and softcover: Coastal Carolina
Published 1999

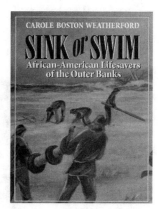

Another little-known chapter in African American history is thoroughly told in this book about the all-black crew of the U.S. Lifesaving Service (forerunner to the U.S. Coast Guard), which operated from 1880 to 1947, from Pea Island off the North Carolina coast. This crew, led by Richard Etheridge, was never recognized for their hundreds of heroic life-saving missions in the hurricane-prone Outer Banks until 1996, when President Clinton honored the brave seamen posthumously with the Coast Guard's esteemed Gold Lifesaving Medal.

THE CREATOR'S

Mildred Pitts Walter

AUTHOR

174

"When I was growing up I had only the Bible to read. I grew up in a small Louisiana town where there was only one library. African Americans were not allowed access to books there. I would have loved any book at that time, and one about people like me would have been a treasure. It was not until I went to college that I had access to lots of books. Seeing hundreds of books on shelves was overwhelming. I didn't know where to start. However, start I did, and I have had a reverence for libraries and books ever since. How I wish the wonderful stories, biographies, historical fiction, and nonfiction by and about African Americans had been available when I was a child."

MILDRED PITTS WALTER

SUITCASE

Illustrated by TERESA FLAVIN

BLACK BOOKS GALORE!

OUR FAVORITES FROM
MILDRED PITTS WALTER

Have a Happy . . . : A Novel about Kwanzaa [296]

Justin and the Best Biscuits in the World [304]

My Mama Needs Me [62]

Suitcase [338]

Two and Too Much [243]

Sky Kings: Black Pioneers of Professional Basketball [332]

Written by Bijan C. Bayne

Softcover: Franklin Watts, Grolier
Published 1997

The game of basketball, invented in 1890 by James Naismith, has become at least as popular as baseball, if not more so. Yet young fans may not know of the history of the sport nor of the black pioneers who opened the game for other African Americans. Young readers will learn about the trials and tribulations of early black players like those on the Harlem Renaissance, the team that won the 1938–39 world championship; and of Chuck Cooper, Earl Lloyd, and Nat Clifton, who were the first to break through the color lines to integrate professional basketball. The book covers select pioneers and their achievements through the 1960s, when African Americans began to dominate the sport.

Smiffy Blue, Ace Crime Detective: The Case of the Missing Ruby and Other Stories [333]

Written by Walter Dean Myers ☆ 112
Illustrated by David J.A. Sims

Hardcover: Scholastic
Published 1996

Smiffy Blue, ace crime detective, and Jeremy Joe, his bumbling sidekick, solve a series of mysteries in this collection of four short stories. Written at a level appropriate for younger readers, each story is illustrated with pictures that have give-away clues that reveal the solution even before Smiffy works it out. Young readers will love the silly stories and Smiffy's sleuthing bloopers in this easy-to-read book.

Sports Report Series [334]

Written by Ron Knapp

Hardcover: Enslow
Published 1994–1996

This biographical series features easy-to-read stories about some of America's greatest sports stars. Each title is complete with high-action photographs, statistics, and interesting factual sidebars about the subject. Nine African American athletes are featured in the series: Charles Barkley, Michael Jordan, Shaquille O'Neal, David Robinson, Barry Sanders, Deion Sanders, Emmitt Smith, Frank Thomas, and Thurman Thomas.

The Spray-Paint Mystery [335]

Written by Angela Shelf Medearis

Softcover: Little Apple, Scholastic
Published 1996

Young Cameron and his best friend, Tarann, are on the trail of the someone who painted graffiti on a school wall. Cameron has honed his detective skills and powers of observation to narrow the suspects down to three possibilities. Now he and Tarann embark on a plan to figure out the puzzling case. Young readers will enjoy trying to second-guess the two young sleuths and figure out the case before the surprising end.

Darryl Tookes reads often to his four children—Christian, 10; Ryann and Channing, 8; and little Tessa, age 2. "Since there is a big age spread between my kids, one day I'm reading picture books and the next day we're checking out biographies of Jesse Owens."

Stealing Home [336]

Written by Mary Stolz

Hardcover and softcover: HarperCollins
Published 1992

The peaceful lifestyle of Thomas and his grandfather is turned upside down when Aunt Linzy comes for an extended visit. Aunt Linzy, a cleaning fanatic, constantly bickers with Grandfather and is not interested in the sports that Grandfather and Thomas hold so dear. Grandfather tries to be patient and encourages Thomas to do the same, but it gets tougher with each passing day. The situation is amusing in this sports-oriented story, full of fast-paced baseball games, and will provide pleasant easy reading for preteens. Other books about Thomas and his grandfather include *Coco Grimes, Go Fish* [293], and *Storm in the Night* [231].

Stuffin' It [337]

Written by Robb Armstrong
Illustrated by Bruce Smith

Softcover: Harper Active, HarperCollins
Published 1998

Twelve-year-old Patrick Ewing and his crew are having the time of their lives. They are rehearsing for the school's Thanksgiving play, which is important because a famous alum, Linc Williams, star of a hit television series, will come to the performance. They are also practicing for an important rematch against one of their rival neighborhood basketball teams. But with all the focus on extracurricular activities, Patrick and his homeboy, Ronnie, let their grades slip. Now they have been put on notice: Get at least a B on the upcoming math test or they will be out of the play and benched for the big game. There are two ways to make the grade—cheat or study—and that is the tough choice that Patrick and Ronnie must make. Other books in the Patrick's Pals series include *Got Game?* [295], *In Your Face* [299], *Large and In Charge!, Runnin' with the Big Dawgs* [328], *Schoolin',* and *Trashmaster* [344].

Suitcase [338]

Written by Mildred Pitts Walter ☆ 174
Illustrated by Teresa Flavin

Hardcover: Lothrop, Lee & Shepard, William Morrow
Published 1999

Eleven-year-old Alexander, also known as "Suitcase" because of his big feet, is over six feet tall and seems like a natural for the basketball court. But Alexander doesn't like basketball at all and would prefer to become an artist. Young Alexander is torn between trying to please his father, who wants him to play ball, and following his own heart. Eventually, Alexander does get the opportunity to demonstrate his artistic ability and makes his father proud of him for his own special gifts.

The Terrible, Wonderful Tellin' at Hog Hammock [339]

Written by Kim Siegelson

Hardcover: HarperCollins
Published 1996

Every year there was a storytelling contest in Hog Hammock, Gullah County. Young Jonas used to go to hear his grandpa, who was the best storyteller around, tell his tales. Now Grandpa is dead. So Grandma decides Jonas must carry on the family tradition. Young readers will relate to the nervous and insecure Jonas, and discover how he finds the strength to perform on his big night. *Nonstandard English.*

Themba [340]

Written by Margaret Sacks
Illustrated by Wil Clay

Softcover: Puffin, Penguin USA
Published 1985

After waiting for three long years, Themba is disappointed and worried when his father does not return as planned from the gold mines outside Johannesburg, where he has been working. Although young, and just a country boy, Themba knows that he must go into town to find his father. Several black-and-white illustrations embellish the short story of Themba's memorable and adventurous journey through modern-day South Africa.

Till Victory Is Won: Black Soldiers in the Civil War [341]

Written by Zak Mettger

Softcover: Puffin, Penguin
Published 1994

A comprehensive history of African Americans' role in the Civil War is described in six fact-filled chapters. The book offers insights into the political climate, the motivation of the Union, and the motivation of blacks themselves during this turbulent time in our history. It also recounts the significant contributions made by blacks and their influence on the outcome of the war. The book is full of illustrations, including some antique photographs from the time.

The Toothpaste Millionaire [342]

Written by Jean Merrill
Illustrated by Jan Palmer

Hardcover and softcover: Houghton Mifflin
Published 1972

Twelve-year-old Rufus Mayflower, amazed by the high cost of an everyday product, begins a profitable enterprise with a classmate to make and distribute a superior and more economical toothpaste. Important principles about business and free enterprise are embedded in this light-hearted story.

Toussaint L'Ouverture: The Fight for Haiti's Freedom [343]

Written by Walter Dean Myers ☆ 112
Illustrated by Jacob Lawrence

Hardcover: Simon & Schuster
Published 1996

Distinguished writer Walter Dean Myers adds meaningful narrative to the renowned series of forty-one provocative tempera paintings created by Jacob Lawrence. The paintings tell the story of Haiti's great liberator, Toussaint L'Ouverture, who fought for the island nation's independence from France in the early 1800s.

Trashmaster [344]

Written by Robb Armstrong
Illustrated by Bruce Smith

Softcover: HarperEntertainment, HarperCollins
Published 1999

A twelve-year-old Patrick Ewing and his friends on the neighborhood basketball team, the Bulldogs, learn that there is more to winning a game of
hoops than good moves. Players also have to be able to talk enough trash to
psych out the competition. Their point is proven when their teammate,
Ronnie, who is known for talking trash, clams up during a game with the
Terminators. He had been humiliated for his poor game skills in a previous
game and decided to shut up until he could "walk the walk." Without
Ronnie's mouth to frustrate the Terminators, the Bulldogs lose. In a rematch,
Ronnie becomes the MVP when he returns to his trash-talking ways. This
story is in the Patrick's Pals series, which features fictionalized stories about
Patrick Ewing and fellow NBA players Dikembe Mutombo and Alonzo
Mourning. Other titles in the series are *Got Game?* [295], *In Your Face* [299],
Large and In Charge!, Runnin' with the Big Dawgs [328], *Schoolin',* and
Stuffin' It [337].

The Watsons Go to Birmingham—1963 [345]

Written by Christopher Paul Curtis

Newbery Honor Book
Coretta Scott King Honor: Author

Hardcover: Delacorte, Bantam Doubleday Dell
Softcover: Yearling Books
Published 1995

Ten-year-old Byron and his family leave their Flint, Michigan, home in an
ultraglide car to visit Grandma in Birmingham, Alabama. Mr. and Mrs.
Watson believe that exposure to the slower-paced lifestyle of the South will be
good for their urban children. Unfortunately, their trip comes in the midst of
the turbulent, racially charged summer of 1963. The Watsons experience the
unfamiliar oppression of segregation, and the supercharged racial hatred of
the deep South. This deeply felt novel will take young readers on a convincing
journey into this dark period in recent American history.

The Well [346]

Written by Mildred D. Taylor

Hardcover: Dial
Published 1995

The Logans, a black family in rural Mississippi in the early 1900s, have the only potable well in the area. They share generously with all of their neighbors, black and white. Despite their kindness, tensions grow between the young Logan boys and their white neighbors, resulting in a potentially explosive situation. Oppressive attitudes about blacks reflective of the South in that era are strongly stated in this book. Other novels about the Logan family include *Roll of Thunder, Hear My Cry; The Road to Memphis; Song of the Trees;* and *Let the Circle Be Unbroken.* **Nonstandard English. Use of N word.**

When I Left My Village [347]

Written by Maxine Ross Schur
Illustrated by Brian Pinkney

Hardcover: Dial
Published 1996

Young Menelik and his family are members of the obscure Beta Israel tribe, the black Jews of Ethiopia. Among their fellow countrymen they are hated and feared. As a people, their burning dream is to return to Israel. When famine, war, and persecution of the Beta Israel reach an intolerable level, the small family decides to make the harrowing journey from Ethiopia to the Sudan, and then on to Israel. If caught, they could be killed just for trying, or they could die of starvation along the way. One way or the other their destiny awaits them. Young readers will learn about a group of black people they never knew in this dramatic story.

Which Way Freedom? [348]

Written by Joyce Hansen   Coretta Scott King Honor: Author

Softcover: Avon Camelot, Avon
Published 1986

Sixteen-year-old Obi, a runaway slave, joins a black division of the Union Army to help fight for the freedom of his people. Obi is a highly principled young man, who is deeply pained by being sold away from his mother. He bravely runs away from his master and fights to help earn freedom and security for himself and his adopted slave family. This fictionalized story is based on actual events and establishes the significant role that runaway slaves played in the Civil War and their personal quest for freedom.

Ziggy and the Black Dinosaurs [349]

Written by Sharon M. Draper ☆ 26
Illustrated by James E. Ransome

Softcover: Just Us
Published 1994

Preteen Ziggy and his three friends—Rico, Rashawn, and Jerome—thought that they were in for a boring summer in this delightfully boyish chapter book. The basketball hoop had been destroyed and the swimming pool had been closed, so there was nothing for the boys to do until they creatively formed their own club, known as the Black Dinosaurs. The four adventurous boys decide to bury their club's secret treasures, leading them to a box of buried bones. Now they have the mystery of their young lives to solve, and that is exactly what they do. Other adventures of the club are found in *Ziggy and the Black Dinosaurs: Lost in the Tunnel of Time* [350] and *Ziggy and the Black Dinosaurs: Shadows of Caesar's Creek*.

Ziggy and the Black Dinosaurs: Lost in the Tunnel of Time [350]

Written by Sharon M. Draper ☆ 26
Illustrated by Michael Bryant

Softcover: Just Us
Published 1996

Ziggy and his friends are intrigued by a lecture about the secret hiding places in their town that used to be a part of the Underground Railroad. The adventurous boys go exploring and discover a trap door that leads to a tunnel under their school that they believe is the threshold to the hidden rooms. The door slams shut and the four are hopelessly trapped and then lost in the dark maze. After several frightening hours and the wild imaginings of the young boys, they are dramatically rescued. Other books in this series include *Ziggy and the Black Dinosaurs* [349] and *Ziggy and the Black Dinosaurs: Shadows of Caesar's Creek*.

BOOKS FOR PARENTS OF BOYS

As a natural extension of our work with African American children's books, we often find books that are particularly interesting to us as parents. We would like to share with you a few of them that apply directly to raising boys.

Boys into Men: Raising Our African American Teenage Sons by Nancy Boyd-Franklin, Ph.D., and A.J. Franklin, Ph.D., with Pamela Toussaint (Dutton Books, 2000). This significant book offers sound, practical advice to the parents of African American boys to help them understand and successfully raise their black sons. The book addresses the proper handling of both the issues that confront boys in general, such as drugs, peer influence, and sex, but also additional problems that challenge African American boys and others in modern society, such as racism, rap music, and violence. The professional advice is backed up by anecdotal cases from dozens of African American families who were counseled by the authors. This thought-provoking book is a thorough guide for concerned parents, complete with extensive lists of other parenting resources.

Success Guideposts for African-American Children: A Guide for Parents of Children Ages 0–18 by Will Horton (W. Whorton & Company, 1998). The objective of this book is to help parents become better teachers—because parents are their children's first and most influential teacher." And it does that well. Parents will receive explicit lessons in developing and nurturing self-confident, motivated, academically inclined children. The advice is sound for any family but specifically tailored to address African American family needs. The book includes step-by-step guidelines for providing positive, uplifting messages to children to enhance their performance in school and in life.

Beating the Odds: Raising Academically Successful African American Males by Freeman A. Hrabowski III, Kenneth I. Maton, and Geoffrey L. Greif

(Oxford University Press, 1998). Confronting the odds against academic success for African American males, this book offers parents a plan to nurture and direct their black sons toward scholastic achievement. Parents will learn the essential strategies for effective parenting: child-focused love, strong limit-setting and discipline, consistent and strong communication, positive racial identity and positive male identity, and full use of community resources. Consistent implementation of these strategies has proven successful in a large cross-section of African American homes—from two-parent to single-parent homes, in a wide range of economic and educational backgrounds. This step-by-step guide offers parents the knowledge necessary to help their sons excel in school in preparation for their promising futures.

Saving Our Sons: Raising Black Children in a Turbulent World by Marita Golden (Doubleday, 1995). Through the story of one mother and her son, other parents can achieve insight into the challenges of raising an African American son. This provocative book eloquently expresses what black parents fear the most—that their sons will fall victim to the societal traps of racism, poor self-esteem, failure, violence, drugs, gangs, and worse. But, through her story and interviews with other black males, from criminals to scholars, and the insights of other writers and psychologists, parents can sort through what must be done to help their sons move through boyhood into productive manhood.

Real Boys: Rescuing Our Sons from the Myths of Boyhood by William Pollack, Ph.D. (Random House, 1998). The author unmasks the young boys in our society who are forced to live behind the image of masculinity that has been cast for them as strong, independent, in-control "little men." This book peels back the layers to look at boys as they really are—sensitive, vulnerable, and insecure—so that parents can better understand, communicate with, and bond with their male children. The book explores the differences and similarities between boys and girls, the emotional burdens that boys bear because they are boys, and how parents and others can help nurture a stronger, more confident young man. This must-read book is followed by *Real Boys' Voices*, which further explores the psychology of the developing young male.

Raising Cain: Protecting the Emotional Life of Boys by Dan Kindlon, Ph.D., and Michael Thompson, Ph.D. (Ballantine Books, 1999). This book offers a disturbing view of the emotional miseducation of boys in our society and the resulting risks of suicide, loneliness, violence, and substance abuse that plague them. This well-researched book reorients parents and others to help raise a better-adjusted young man who embraces rather than rejects qualities like compassion, sensitivity, and warmth. After a thorough look at everything that is wrong with our boy-rearing culture and the unfortunate consequences, the good news is that there is a chapter titled "What Boys Need," which offers seven recommendations for raising happier, healthier sons.

INDEX OF TITLES

Italic type indicates a book that is mentioned only within the main entry or entries listed.
Bold type indicates the name of a series, not the title of an individual book.

Baby–Preschool [1–85]   K–Grade 3 [86–260]   Grades 4–8 [261–350]

INDEX OF AUTHORS

INDEX OF ILLUSTRATORS

INDEX OF TOPICS

baby (new)

Daniel's Dog [18]
Everett Anderson's Nine Month Long [24]
My Mama Needs Me [62]
On the Day I Was Born [65]
One Round Moon and a Star for Me [207]
Peter's Chair [67]
She Come Bringing Me That Little Baby Girl [73]
Silver Rain Brown [225]
Something Special [78]
Will There Be a Lap for Me? [84]

baby's day

Animal Sounds for Baby [1]
The Baby [2]
Baby Says [3]
Baby's Bedtime [4]
Billy's Boots: A First Lift-the-Flap Book [9]
Oh, No, Toto! [64]
Simeon's Sandbox [74]

babysitters

What Kind of Baby-Sitter Is This? [249]

baseball. *see* sports

basketball. *see* sports

beach

The Boy on the Beach [106]
Joshua by the Sea [51]

bedtime

Golden Bear [32]
Good Night Baby [33]
Joshua's Night Whispers [52]

bible stories. *see* religion

biography

Alvin Ailey [87]
Anthony Burns: The Defeat and Triumph of a Fugitive Slave [265]
At the Plate with Ken Griffey, Jr. [267]
Black Cowboy, Wild Horses: A True Story [102]
Coming Home: From the Life of Langston Hughes [114]
Dear Benjamin Banneker [119]
Denzel Washington: Actor [278]
Duke Ellington: The Piano Prince and His Orchestra [120]
Escape to Freedom: A Play about Young Frederick Douglass [283]
First in the Field: Baseball Hero Jackie Robinson [286]
Frederick Douglass: The Last Days of Slavery [288]
Free to Dream: The Making of a Poet, Langston Hughes [289]
From Slave to Civil War Hero: The Life and Times of Robert Smalls [291]
Happy Birthday, Dr. King! [140]
Happy Birthday, Martin Luther King [141]
I Have a Dream: Dr. Martin Luther King, Jr. [150]
If I Only Had a Horn: Young Louis Armstrong [151]
Kobe Bryant [165]
Leagues Apart: The Men and Times of the Negro Baseball Leagues [169]
Leon's Story [308]
Malcolm X [177]
Male Writers [310]
Mandela: From the Life of the South African Statesman [178]
Meet Martin Luther King, Jr.: A Man of Peace with a Dream for All People [181]
More Than Anything Else [186]
My Dream of Martin Luther King [189]
My Name Is York [194]

On the Course with Tiger Woods [318]
On the Court with Grant Hill [319]
On the Field with Emmitt Smith [320]
A Picture Book of Thurgood Marshall [212]
The Real McCoy: The Life of an African-American Inventor [217]
Satchmo's Blues [221]
The Story of Jean Baptiste DuSable [232]
Teammates [239]
Toussaint L'Ouverture: The Fight for Haiti's Freedom [343]
A Weed Is a Flower: The Life of George Washington Carver [248]

birthday

Birthday [101]
Jackson Jones and the Puddle of Thorns [154]
Uh-oh! It's Mama's Birthday! [80]

Caribbean

The Crab Man [115]
The Faithful Friend [124]
Gregory Cool [138]
The House in the Sky: A Bahamian Folktale [146]
Hue Boy [148]
Island Baby [43]
My Little Island [190]
Tukama Tootles the Flute: A Tale from the Antilles [79]

Christmas. *see* holidays

church. *see* religion

city life

The Boy Who Didn't Believe in Spring [107]
Granddaddy's Street Songs [134]
Somewhere in Africa [228]

civil rights

I Have a Dream: Dr. Martin Luther King, Jr. [150]
Let Freedom Ring: A Ballad of Martin Luther King, Jr. [170]

Civil War

Abraham's Battle: A Novel of Gettysburg [261]
Across the Lines [262]
The Blue and the Gray [104]
Pink and Say [321]
Silent Thunder: A Civil War Story [330]
Till Victory Is Won: Black Soldiers in the Civil War [341]

conjure. *see* magic

cousins. *see* siblings

cowboys. *see* pioneers

dance

Alvin Ailey [87]
Brothers of the Knight [109]
Dance [17]
How Many Stars in the Sky? [147]

death

The Day I Saw My Father Cry [117]
The New King: A Madagascan Legend [200]

disability

Brian's Bird [108]

family life/situations

Because You're Lucky [93]
The Bells of Christmas [94]
Charlie's House [12]
Daddy and I [15]
Daddy Calls Me Man [16]
Evan's Corner [123]

Everett Anderson's 1-2-3 [25]
Everett Anderson's Nine Month Long [24]
Father and Son [27]
First Pink Light [127]
Gettin' Through Thursday [132]
Grandma's Hands [135]
Grandpa's Visit [137]
Hanging Out with Mom [38]
How Many Stars in the Sky? [147]
I Love My Family [41]
Jafta's Mother [46]
Jamal's Busy Day [48]
Keepers [162]
Kevin and His Dad [164]
The Longest Wait [174]
Ma Dear's Aprons [175]
Me and My Family Tree [59]
My Mama Needs Me [62]
My Man Blue [192]
My Mom Is My Show-and-Tell [193]
One Round Moon and a Star for Me [207]
Poppa's Itchy Christmas [214]
Read for Me, Mama [216]
Robert Lives with His Grandparents [219]
Sam [71]
Stevie [229]
The Worst Day of My Life [257]
Your Dad Was Just Like You [258]

fantasy

The Adventures of Sparrowboy [86]
Bear on a Bike [5]
Big Boy [7]
Daniel's Dog [18]
Dave and the Tooth Fairy [19]
Kofi and the Butterflies [53]
A Million Fish . . . More or Less [182]

fears

Kele's Secret [163]
One Dark and Scary Night [206]

folktales, fairy tales and legends

African

Anansi Finds a Fool [89]
The Fortune-Tellers [129]
Gift of the Sun: A Tale from South Africa [133]
The Hatseller and the Monkeys [143]
Koi and the Kola Nuts: A Tale from Liberia [167]
The Magic Tree: A Folktale from Nigeria [176]
Nobiah's Well: A Modern African Folktale [202]
The Orphan Boy [209]
Palampam Day [66]
Sebgugugu the Glutton: A Bantu Tale from Rwanda, Africa [222]
The Singing Man: Adapted from a West African Folktale [226]
Sundiata: Lion King of Mali [236]
What's So Funny, Ketu? [250]

American

Big Jabe [96]
The Boy and the Ghost [105]
The Hired Hand: An African American Folktale [144]
Imani and the Flying Africans [152]
In the Time of the Drums [153]
Jake and Honeybunch Go to Heaven [47]
John Henry [156]
Little Muddy Waters: A Gullah Folk Tale [173]
Rumplestiltskin [70]
Sam and the Tigers: A New Retelling of Little Black Sambo [220]
Shaq and the Beanstalk: And Other Very Tall Tales [224]
Tailypo! [238]
Wiley and the Hairy Man [252]

Caribbean

The Faithful Friend [124]

The House in the Sky: A Bahamian Folktale [146]

Tukama Tootles the Flute: A Tale from the Antilles [79]

football. *see* sports

friendship with adults

Elijah's Angel: A Story for Chanukah and Christmas [121]

Miss Viola and Uncle Ed Lee [183]

friendship with peers

Big Friend, Little Friend [8]
The Blue and the Gray [104]
Creativity [116]
Everett Anderson's Friend [23]
My Best Friend [61]
Somebody's New Pajamas [227]

games and riddles

The Barber's Cutting Edge [90]

gardening/farming

Jackson Jones and the Puddle of Thorns [154]
Max Loves Sunflowers [56]

grandparents

Bigmama's [97]
Fireflies for Nathan [126]
Go Fish [293]
Granddaddy's Street Songs [134]
Grandfather and I [34]
Grandfather's Work: A Traditional Healer in Nigeria [35]
Grandma's Hands [135]
Grandpa, Is Everything Black Bad? [136]
Grandpa's Visit [137]
Justin and the Best Biscuits in the World [304]
Keepers [162]

One Dark and Scary Night [206]
Robert Lives with His Grandparents [219]
Stealing Home [336]
Storm in the Night [231]
The Treasure Hunt [241]
When I Am Old with You [82]
When I Was Little [251]
William and the Good Old Days [253]

Gullah Islands

Imani and the Flying Africans [152]
In the Time of the Drums [153]
Little Muddy Waters: A Gullah Folk Tale [173]
A Net to Catch Time [199]

hair

An Enchanted Hair Tale [122]
Haircuts at Sleepy Sam's [139]

history/heritage/historical fiction

Come All You Brave Soldiers: Blacks in the Revolutionary War [276]
If You Please, President Lincoln [298]
Just Like Martin [303]
Mississippi Chariot [314]
Sink or Swim: African-American Lifesavers of the Outer Banks [331]
Till Victory Is Won: Black Soldiers in the Civil War [341]
Tommy Traveler in the World of Black History [240]
The Watsons Go to Birmingham— 1963 [345]
Which Way Freedom? [348]

holidays

Christmas
An Angel Just Like Me [88]
The Bells of Christmas [94]
Calvin's Christmas Wish [111]

Elijah's Angel: A Story for Chanukah and Christmas [121]
The Freedom Riddle [130]
O Christmas Tree [203]
Poppa's Itchy Christmas [214]

Halloween
Halloween Monster [37]

Kwanzaa
Have A Happy . . . : A Novel about Kwanzaa [296]
Wood-Hoopoe Willie [256]

Valentine's Day
Super-Fine Valentine [237]

Kwanzaa. *see* holidays

legends. *see* folktales

literacy

More Than Anything Else [186]
Read for Me, Mama [216]
Richard Wright and the Library Card [218]

magic (conjure)

Wiley and the Hairy Man [252]

music/musicians

The Bat Boy and His Violin [91]
Charlie Parker Played Be Bop [11]
Duke Ellington: The Piano Prince and His Orchestra [120]
If I Only Had a Horn: Young Louis Armstrong [151]
Max Found Two Sticks [179]
The Music in Derrick's Heart [187]
My Mama Sings [191]
The Old Cotton Blues [204]
Ty's One-Man Band [244]
Willie Jerome [254]
Wood-Hoopoe Willie [256]

mystery

Ghost Train [292]
Gold Diggers [294]
Jimmy Lee Did It [155]
Kid Caramel, Private Investigator: Case of the Missing Ankh [305]
Kid Caramel, Private Investigator: The Werewolf of PS 40 [306]
Smiffy Blue, Ace Crime Detective: The Case of the Missing Ruby and Other Stories [333]
The Spray-Paint Mystery [335]

pets/animals

Bear on a Bike [5]
Bimmi Finds a Cat [100]
Brian's Bird [108]
Digby [21]
Get the Ball, Slim [30]
Honey Hunters [39]
Island Baby [43]
Kofi and the Butterflies [53]
Lake of the Big Snake: An African Rain Forest Adventure [168]
Max [55]
Willie's Wonderful Pet [85]

pioneers and cowboys

Adventures of Midnight Son [263]
Bill Pickett: Rodeo-Ridin' Cowboy [98]
Black Cowboy, Wild Horses: A True Story [102]
Buffalo Soldiers: The Story of Emanuel Stance [110]
The Journal of Joshua Loper: A Black Cowboy, The Chisholm Trail, 1871 [300]
The Longest Ride [309]
A Pony for Jeremiah [323]
Reflections of a Black Cowboy: Pioneers [325]
The Righteous Revenge of Artemis Bonner [326]
Wagon Wheels [247]

playtime

The Best Way to Play [95]
From My Window [28]
Sharing Danny's Dad [72]

poetry (rhymes)

Bringing the Rain to Kapiti Plain [10]
Daddy Calls Me Man [16]
Everett Anderson's 1-2-3 [23]
Everett Anderson's Friend [24]
Everett Anderson's Nine Month Long [25]
Everett Anderson's Year [26]
For the Love of the Game: Michael Jordan and Me [128]
Free to Dream: The Making of a Poet, Langston Hughes [289]
Kevin and His Dad [164]
Let Freedom Ring: A Ballad of Martin Luther King, Jr. [170]
Me and My Family Tree [59]
Mighty Menfolk [60]
My Man Blue [192]
Nathaniel Talking [196]
Red Dog, Blue Fly: Football Poems [324]
Some of the Days of Everett Anderson [77]

preschool skills

colors

Chidi Only Likes Blue: An African Book of Colors [13]

counting

Emeka's Gift: An African Counting Story [22]
Joe Can Count [49]

words

Furaha Means Happy!: A Book of Swahili Words [29]
Halala Means Welcome!: A Book of Zulu Words [36]

religion

Bible stories

Climbing Jacob's Ladder: Heroes of the Bible in African-American Spirituals [14]
Noah [63]

Jewish

Elijah's Angel: A Story for Chanukah and Christmas [121]
When I Left My Village [347]

responsibility

I Can Do It by Myself [149]
Jackson Jones and the Puddle of Thorns [154]
Kevin and His Dad [164]
The Paperboy [211]

rhymes. *see* poetry

riddles. *see* games

role model

For the Love of the Game: Michael Jordan and Me [128]
Mighty Menfolk [60]
My Man Blue [192]

school

Be Patient, Abdul [92]
My Mom Is My Show-and-Tell [193]
A School for Pompey Walker [329]
Willie's Wonderful Pet [85]

seasons/weather

The Boy Who Didn't Believe in Spring [107]
Drylongso [282]
Everett Anderson's Year [26]
From My Window [28]
The Longest Wait [174]
Silver Rain Brown [225]
Snow on Snow on Snow [75]

PERMISSIONS AND CREDITS

The following illustrations are reprinted with permission:

Page 13: Cover illustration by E. B. Lewis from *Big Boy* by Tololwa M. Mollel. Copyright © 1995. Reprinted by permission of Clarion Books/Houghton Mifflin.

Page 14: From *Charlie Parker Played Be Bop* (jacket cover) by Chris Raschka. Copyright © 1992 by Christopher Raschka. Reprinted by permission of the publisher, Orchard Books, New York.

Page 16: Cover photograph by Susan Kuklin from *Dance* by Bill T. Jones and Susan Kuklin. Copyright © 1998. Reprinted by permission of Hyperion.

Pages 19, 53: Cover illustration by E. B. Lewis from *The Bat Boy and His Violin* by Gavin Curtis. Copyright © 1998. Courtesy of Simon & Schuster Books for Young Readers, an imprint of Simon & Schuster Children's Publishing.

Page 21: From *Everett Anderson's Nine Month Long* (jacket cover) by Lucille Clifton, illustrated by Ann Grifalconi. Text copyright © 1978 by Lucille Clifton. Illustrations copyright © 1978 by Ann Grifalconi. Reprinted by permission of Henry Holt & Co., LLC.

Page 22: From *Everett Anderson's Year* (jacket cover) by Lucille Clifton, illustrated by Ann Grifalconi. Text copyright © 1974 by Lucille Clifton. Illustrations copyright, © 1974 by Ann Grifalconi. Reprinted by permission of Henry Holt & Co., LLC.

Page 24: Cover illustration by Jan Ormerod from *Grandfather and I* by Helen E. Buckley. Jacket illustration copyright © 1994. Reprinted by permission of Lothrop, Lee & Shepard, William Morrow & Company, Inc.

Pages 27, 183: Cover illustration from *Ziggy and the Black Dinosaurs: Lost in the Tunnel of Time* by Sharon Draper. Copyright © 1996. Reprinted by permission of Just Us Books.

Page 28: Cover illustration by Fred Willingham from *I Can Count* by Denise

Lewis Patrick. Copyright © 1996. Reprinted by permission of Essence Books.

Page 29: From *Jafta and the Wedding* (jacket cover) by Hugh Lewin, illustrations by Lisa Kopper. Copyright 1983 by Carol Rhoda Books, Inc. Used by permission of the publisher. All rights reserved.

Page 30: From *Jafta's Mother* (jacket cover) by Hugh Lewin, illustrations by Lisa Kopper. Copyright 1983 by Carol Rhoda Books, Inc. Used by permission of the publisher. All rights reserved.

Page 31: Cover illustration by George Ford from *Jamal's Busy Day* by Wade Hudson. Cover illustration copyright © 1991 by George Ford. Reprinted by permission of Just Us Books.

Page 32: Cover illustration by Michael Hays from *Jonathan and His Mommy* by Irene Smalls. Illustration copyright © 1992 by Michael Hays. Reprinted by permission of Little, Brown & Company.

Page 34: Cover illustration from *Max Loves Sunflowers* by Ken Wilson-Max. Copyright © 1998. Reprinted by permission of Hyperion. Cover illustration from *Max's Money* by Ken Wilson-Max. Copyright © 1999. Reprinted by permission of Jump at the Sun, Hyperion.

Pages 35, 59: Cover illustration by Cornelius Van Wright from *My Best Friend* by P. Mignon Hinds. Illustrations copyright © 1997 by Cornelius Van Wright. Reprinted by permission of Essence Books.

Page 40: Cover illustration by Cathy Johnson from *Robo's Favorite Places* by Wade Hudson. Copyright © 1999. Reprinted by permission of Just Us Books.

Pages 47, 65: From *When I Am Old with You* (jacket cover) by Angela Johnson, illustrated by David Soman. Text © 1990 by Angela Johnson. Illustration © 1990 by David Soman. Reprinted by permission of the publisher, Orchard Books, New York.

Page 47: Cover illustration by Nina Crews from *When Will Sarah Come?* by Elizabeth Fitzgerald. Copyright © 1999. Reprinted by permission of William

Morrow & Company, Inc. Cover illustration by Nancy Poydar from *Will There Be a Lap for Me?* by Dorothy Corey. Jacket illustration copyright © 1992 by Nancy Poydar. Reprinted by permission of Albert Whitman & Company.

Page 48: Illustration by George Ford from *Willie's Wonderful Pet* (jacket cover) by Mel Cebulash. Illustration copyright © 1993 by George Ford. Reprinted by permission of Scholastic Inc.

Page 52: Cover illustration by Raymond Holbert from *The Barber's Cutting Edge* by Gwendolyn Battle-Lavert. Reprinted with permission of the publisher, Children's Book Press, San Francisco, CA. Story copyright © 1997 by Gwendolyn Battle-Levert, illustrations copyright © 1997 by Raymond Holbert.

Page 53: Cover illustration by Michael Hays from *Because You're Lucky* by Irene Smalls. Copyright © 1997. Reprinted by permission of Little, Brown.

Page 55: Cover illustration from *Bigmama's* by Donald Crews. Copyright © 1991. Reprinted by permission of Greenwillow. Cover illustration by Brian Pinkney from *Bill Pickett: Rodeo-Ridin' Cowboy* by Andrea Davis Pinkney. Jacket illustration copyright © 1996 by Brian Pinkney. Reproduced by permission of Harcourt Inc.

Page 57: Illustration by Carole Byard from *The Black Snowman* (jacket cover) by Phil Mendez. Illustration copyright © 1989 by Carole Byard. Reprinted by permission of Scholastic Inc.

Page 60: Cover illustration from *The Boy on the Beach* by Niki Daly. Copyright © 1999. Courtesy of Margaret K. McElderberry Books, an imprint of Simon & Schuster Children's Publishing.

Page 62: Cover illustration by Roy Condy from *Christopher, Please Clean Up Your Room!* by Itah Sadu. Copyright © 1993. Reprinted by permission of Firefly Press.

Page 63: Cover illustration from *Clean*

Your Room, Harvey Moon! by Pat Cummings. Copyright © 1991. Courtesy of Simon & Schuster Books for Young Readers, an imprint of Simon & Schuster Children's Publishing.

Page 66: Illustration by Varnette P. Honeywood from *The Day I Was Rich* (jacket cover) by Bill Cosby Little Bill Books for Beginning Readers published by Cartwheel Books, a division of Scholastic Inc. Copyright © 1999 by Bill Cosby. Reprinted by permission. Cartwheel Books is a registered trademark of Scholastic Inc.

Page 67: Book cover from *Dear Benjamin Banneker* by Andrea Davis Pinkney, jacket illustration copyright © 1994 by Brian Pinkney, reproduced by permission of Harcourt, Inc. Cover illustration by Brian Pinkney from *Duke Ellington: The Piano Prince and His Orchestra* by Andrea Davis Pinkney. Copyright © 1998. Reprinted by permission of Hyperion.

Page 74: Cover illustration by Nneka Bennett from *Gettin' Through Thursday* by Melrose Cooper. Illustration copyright © 1998 by Nneka Bennett. Permission granted by Lee & Low Books, Inc., 95 Madison Avenue New York, NY 10016.

Page 75: Cover illustration by Floyd Cooper from *Granddaddy's Street Songs* by Monalisa DeGross. Copyright © 1999. Reprinted by permission of Jump at the Sun, Hyperion.

Page 78: From *The Hatseller and the Monkeys* (jacket cover) by Baba Wagué Diakité. Published by Scholastic Press, a division of Scholastic Inc. Copyright © 1999 by Baba Wagué Diakité. Reprinted by permission.

Page 79: Cover illustration by James E. Ransome from *How Many Stars in the Sky?* by Lenny Hort. Copyright © 1991. Reprinted by permission of Tambourine Books, a division of William Morrow & Company, Inc.

Page 83: Cover illustration by Leonard Jenkins from *If I Only Had a Horn: Young Louis Armstrong* by Roxane Orgill. Copyright © 1997. Reprinted by permission of Houghton Mifflin.

Page 84: Cover illustration by Brian Pinkney from *In the Time of the Drums* by Kim L. Siegelson. Copyright © 1999.

Reprinted by permission of Jump at the Sun, Hyperion. Cover illustration by Melodye Rosales from *Jackson Jones and the Puddle of Thorns* by Mary Quattlebaum. Copyright © 1994. Reprinted by permission of Delacorte Press Books for Young Readers, a division of Random House, Inc.

Page 85: Cover illustration by Anna Rich from *Joshua's Masai Mask* by Dakari Hru. Illustration copyright © 1993 by Anna Rich. Permission granted by Lee & Low Books, Inc., 95 Madison Avenue, NewYork, NY 10016.

Page 87: Cover illustration by Felicia Marshall from *Keepers* by Jeri Hanel Watts. Illustration copyright © 1997 by Felicia Marshall. Permission granted by Lee & Low Books, Inc., 95 Madison Avenue, New York, NY 10016.

Pages 89, 108: Cover illustration by Cedric Lucas from *Night Golf* by William Miller. Illustration copyright © 1999 by Cedric Lucas. Permission granted by Lee & Low Books, Inc., 95 Madison Avenue New York, NY 10016.

Pages 90, 161: Cover illustration by Michael Hays from *Kevin and His Dad* by Irene Smalls. Copyright © 1999. Reprinted by permission of Little, Brown.

Page 91: Cover illustration by Joe Cepeda from *Koi and the Kola Nuts: A Tale from Liberia* by Verna Aardema. Copyright © 1999. Courtesy of Atheneum Books for Young Readers, an imprint of Simon & Schuster Children's Publishing.

Page 92: Cover illustration by Richard Merkin from *Leagues Apart: The Men and Times of the Negro Baseball Leagues* by Lawrence Ritter. Copyright © 1995. Reprinted by permission of Mulberry, William Morrow & Company, Inc.

Page 95: From *The Longest Wait* (jacket cover) by Marie Bradby, illustrated by Peter Catalanotto. Text © 1998 by Marie Bradby. Illustrations © 1998 by Peter Catalanotto. Reprinted by permission of the publisher, Orchard Books, New York. Cover illustration by Floyd Cooper from *Ma Dear's Aprons* by Patrick McKissack. Copyright © 1997. Courtesy of Atheneum Books for Young Readers/ An Anne Schwartz Book, an imprint of Simon & Schuster Children's Publishing. Cover illustration by E. B. Lewis

from *The Magic Tree: A Folktale from Nigeria* by T. Obinkaram Echewa. Copyright © 1999. Reprinted by permission of William Morrow & Company, Inc.

Page 98: Cover illustration from *Max Found Two Sticks* by Brian Pinkney. Copyright © 1994. Courtesy of Simon & Schuster Books for Young Readers, an imprint of Simon & Schuster Children's Publishing.

Page 100: Cover illustration by Catherine Stock from *Miss Viola and Uncle Ed Lee* by Alice Faye Duncan. Copyright © 1997. Courtesy of Atheneum Books for Young Readers, an imprint of Simon & Schuster Children's Publishing.

Page 111: Illustration by Varnette P. Honeywood from *One Dark and Scary Night* (jacket cover) by Bill Cosby Little Bill Books for Beginning Readers published by Cartwheel Books, a division of Scholastic Inc. Copyright © 1999 by Bill Cosby. Reprinted by permission. Cartwheel Books is a registered trademark of Scholastic Inc.

Page 115: From *The Paperboy* (jacket cover) by Dav Pilkey. Copyright © 1996 by Dav Pilkey. Reprinted by permission of the publisher, Orchard Books, New York. Cover illustration by Robert Casilla from *A Picture Book of Thurgood Marshall* by David A. Adler. Copyright © 1997. Reprinted by permission of Holiday House. Cover illustration by Dan Brown from *A Picture Book of George Washington Carver* by David A. Adler. Copyright © 1999. Reprinted by permission of Holiday House.

Page 117: Illustration by Wil Clay from *The Real McCoy: The Story of an African American Inventor* (jacket cover) by Wendy S. Towle. Illustration copyright © 1999 by Wil Clay. Reprinted by permission of Scholastic Inc.

Page 118: Cover illustration by Gregory Christie from *Richard Wright and the Library Card* by William Miller. Illustration copyright © 1997 by Gregory Christie. Permission granted by Lee & Low Books, Inc., 95 Madison Avenue, New York, NY 10016.

Page 122: Illustration by Shane W. Evans from *Shaq and the Beanstalk* (jacket cover) by Shaquille O'Neal. Published by Cartwheel Books, a division of Scholastic

Inc. Illustration copyright © 1999 by Shane W. Evans. Reprinted by permission. Cartwheel Books is a registered trademark of Scholastic Inc. Cover illustration by Teresa Flavin from *Silver Rain Brown* by M. C. Helldorfer. Copyright © 1999. Reprinted by permission of Houghton Mifflin.

Page 125: Cover illustration by Melodye Benson Rosales from *A Strawbeater's Thanksgiving* by Irene Smalls. Copyright © 1998. Reprinted by permission of Little, Brown.

Page 127: Illustration by Varnette P. Honeywood from *Super-Fine Valentine* (jacket cover) by Bill Cosby Little Bill Books for Beginning Readers published by Cartwheel Books, a division of Scholastic Inc. Copyright © 1998 by Bill Cosby. Reprinted by permission. Cartwheel is a registered trademark of Scholastic Inc.

Pages 129, 153: Cover illustration from *Forty Acres and Maybe a Mule* by Harriette Gillem Robinet. Copyright © 1996. Courtesy of Atheneum Books for Young Readers, an imprint of Simon & Schuster Children's Publishing.

Page 133: Cover illustration by James E. Ransome from *The Wagon* by Tony Johnston. Copyright © 1996. Reprinted by permission of Tambourine Books, a division of William Morrow & Company, Inc.

Page 137: Illustration by Varnette P. Honeywood from *The Worst Day of My Life* (jacket cover) by Bill Cosby Little Bill Books for Beginning Readers published by Cartwheel Books, a division of Scholastic Inc. Copyright © 1999 by Bill Cosby. Reprinted by permission. Cartwheel Books is a reigistered trademark of Scholastic Inc.

Page 148: Cover illustration from *Bud, Not Buddy* by Christopher Paul Curtis. Copyright © 1999. Reprinted by permission of Delacorte Press Books for Young Readers, a division of Random House, Inc.

Page 149: Illustration by John Thompson from *Come All You Brave Soldiers: Blacks in the Revolutionary War* (jacket cover) by Clinton Cox. Published by Scholastic Press, a division of Scholastic Inc. Jacket illustration copyright © 1998 by John Thompson. Reprinted by permission.

Page 150: Cover illustration from *Denzel Washington* (Black Americans of Achievement series) by Anne Hill. Copyright © 1990. Courtesy of Chelsea House Publishers. Cover illustration from *Alex Haley* (Black Americans of Achievement series) by David Shirley. Copyright © 1993. Courtesy of Chelsea House Publishers. Cover illustration from *Thurgood Marshall* (Black Americans of Achievement series) by Lisa Aldred. Copyright © 1990 by Chelsea House Publishers. Reprinted with permission. Cover illustration from *Josh Gibson* (Black Americans of Achievement series) by John B. Holway. Copyright © 1995. Courtesy of Chelsea House Publishers. Cover illustration from *Romare Bearden* (Black Americans of Achievement series) by Kevin Brown. Copyright © 1995. Courtesy of Chelsea House Publishers.

Page 152: From *Fair Ball!* (jacket cover) by Jonah Winter. Published by Scholastic Press, a division of Scholastic Inc. Copyright © 1999 by Jonah Winter. Reprinted by permission.

Page 153: Cover illustration from *First in the Field: Baseball Hero Jackie Robinson* by Derek T. Dingle. Copyright © 1998. Reprinted by permission of Hyperion.

Page 154: Cover illustration from *Free to Dream: The Making of a Poet, Langston Hughes* by Audrey Osofsky. Copyright © 1996. Reprinted by permission of Lothrop, Lee & Shepard, a division of William Morrow & Company, Inc.

Page 162: Cover illustration from *Junebug and the Reverend* by Alice Mead. Copyright © 1998. Reprinted by permission of Farrar, Straus & Giroux. Cover illustration by Catherine Stock from *Justin and the Best Biscuits in the World* by Mildred Pitts Walter. Copyright © 1986. Reprinted by permission of Lothrop, Lee & Shepard, a division of William Morrow & Company, Inc.

Page 165: Cover illustration by Malcah Zeldis from *Martin Luther King* by Rosemary L. Bray. Copyright © 1995. Reprinted by permission of William Morrow & Company, Inc.

Page 168: Cover photograph from *On the Course with Tiger Woods* by Matt Christopher. Copyright © 1998. Reprinted by permission of Little, Brown. Cover photograph from *On the Court with Grant Hill* by Matt Christopher. Copyright © 1991. Reprinted by permission of Little, Brown.

Page 172: Book cover from *A School for Pompey Walker* by Michael J. Rosen, jacket illustration copyright © 1995 by Aminah Brenda Lynn Robinson, reproduced by permission of Harcourt, Inc.

Page 173: Cover illustration by Jerry Pinkney from *Silent Thunder: A Civil War Story* by Andrea Davis Pinkney. Copyright © 1999. Reprinted by permission of Hyperion Books for Children. Cover illustration from *Sink or Swim: African-American Lifesavers of the Outer Banks*. Jacket illustration copyright © 1999. Reprinted by permission of Coastal Carolina Press.

Pages 175, 179: Cover illustration by Teresa Flavin from *Suitcase* by Mildred Pitts Walter. Copyright © 1999. Reprinted by permission of Lothrop, Lee & Shepard, William Morrow & Company, Inc.

Photo Credits:

Photos of the Creators as adults: P. 18, Andrea Curtis; p. 36, Dianne Johnson Feelings; p. 58, N. Stephen Chin; p. 72, Elizabeth King; p. 80, Milan Sabatini.

The photos of the Creators as children were provided by the kind courtesy of the Creators themselves.

Photos of the young readers and their families: Pp. 17, 44, 71, 93, 126, 143, 157, 177, B. D. Parker; p. 109, Anderson's Photography.

ABOUT THE AUTHORS

Donna Rand

Ms. Rand joined *Black Books Galore!* in 1992 as the next step in her search for great books to read to her baby daughter and ten-year-old son. An executive who quit her job to raise her children, she brought to her new mission the formidable professional skills she honed as MCI Telecommunications' former director of service marketing and as a longtime marketing manager at Xerox Corporation.

Ms. Rand lives in Stamford, Connecticut, with her husband and two school-age children.

Toni Trent Parker

Ms. Parker is a graduate of Oberlin College and did graduate work in Black Studies at the University of California, Berkeley. Ms. Parker's professional credentials include service as program officer for the Phelps-Stokes Fund.

A founding member of the Black Family Cultural Exchange, Ms. Parker lives in Stamford, Connecticut, with her husband and three daughters. She is active in a variety of civic organizations.